THE ISLAMIC INVASION

Confronting the World's Fastest Growing Religion

ROBERT MOREY

Christian Scholars Press

1350 E. Flamingo Rd. Suite 97
Las Vegas, NV. 88119

Revised and expanded edition of the book formerly titled *Islam Unveiled*.

THE ISLAMIC INVASION

Copyright © 1992 by Robert A. Morey
Published by Christian Scholars Press
1350 E. Flamingo Rd. Suite 97
Las Vegas, NV. 88119

ISBN 1-931230-07-2

Printed in the United States of America.

Contents

About the Author

Dr. Morey is the Executive Director of the Research and Education Foundation and the author of over forty books, some of which have been translated into French, German, Italian, Polish, Finnish, Dutch, Spanish, Norwegian, Swedish, and Chinese. He is an internationally recognized scholar in the fields of philosophy, theology, comparative religion, the cults and the occult. For more information on his books, audiotapes, and videotapes, write to: The Research and Education Foundation, P.O. Box 7447 Orange, CA 92863 (1-800-41-Truth). He has also written:

The Trinity
Fearing God
Satan's Devices
The Islamic Invasion
The Truth About Masons
Death and the Afterlife
Battle of the Gods
How to Keep Your Faith While in College
The New Atheism and the Erosion of Freedom
An Introduction to Defending the Faith
An Analysis of the Hadith
When Is It Right to Fight?
How to Answer a Jehovah's Witness
How to Answer a Mormon
Reincarnation and Christianity
Horoscopes and the Christian
Worship Is All of Life
How to Keep Your Kids Drug-Free
An Examination of Exclusive Psalmody
Is Allah Just Another Name for God?
Here Is Your God
The Reformation View of Roman Catholicism
Is the Sabbath for Today?
The Dooyeweerdian Concept of the Word of God
The New Life Notebook, Vol. I
The New Life Notebook, Vol. II
The Mood-god Allah in the Archeology of the Middle East

Islam is not only the dominant religion in North Africa, but it is also the second-largest religion in the world, second only to Christianity!

Western Europe

Due to liberal immigration policies, millions of Muslims have now emigrated to the West in search of a better life.

Thus in many Western "Christian" nations, Islam has become the second-largest religion. For example, in France and Germany the Muslims now number in the millions.

The United Kingdom

In England the situation is amazing: There are now more Arab Muslims in England than there are Methodists! There are even more Muslims than there are evangelical Christians.

Funded by the vast resources of Arab oil money, the Muslims are buying abandoned Anglican churches and turning them into mosques at such a rate that some Muslims claim that England will be the first Muslim European country.

The legal situation has reached the point where the English Parliament has been forced to rule that Muslims do not have to follow English Common Law when it comes to such things as divorce; they can follow Islamic law instead.

Australia

Islam has grown from a mere 800 Muslims in 1955 to well over 200,000 by 1990. The influx of Arab emigrants is increasing at a steady rate.

In a lecture tour in the fall of 1989, we found large mosques in all the major cities. There are now more Muslims in the State of Victoria than Baptists.

North America

In North America there are now over 4 million Muslims. Some researchers claim that there are now more Muslims than Jews in North America, which would make Islam the second-largest religion in the United States and Canada.

The United States

Over 500 Islamic centers have been built in the United States. Two-thirds of American Muslims are of Arab descent, while one-third is composed of various black Muslim cults.

There are now officially more Muslims than Episcopalians in the United States.[1]

Extravagant Claims

A word must be said about the extravagant claims by some Muslims that there are as many as 10 to 25 million Muslims in the United States.

On February 22, 1991, I was on a radio talk show with a representative of the Islamic Information Center of America. During the program he claimed that there were over 2 billion Muslims in the world and over 10 million in the United States.

When I asked him for some kind of written documentation for these numbers, he did not provide any.

When I pointed out that the encyclopedias, almanacs, newspapers, and such magazines as _Time_, _Newsweek_, etc. estimate that there are only between 3 and 4 million Muslims in the U.S., and not 10 million as he claimed, the Muslim representative responded by claiming that all the newspapers, encyclopedias, almanacs, magazines, etc. were wrong!

We will stick with the standard reference works until the Muslims can come up with some kind of hard documentation to the contrary.[2]

For example, the 1989 _Almanac_ states that there are only 2.6 million Muslims in North America and only 860 million Muslims worldwide.[3]

Even if we add a million to that total to bring us to 1991 figures, this is still a far cry from Muslim claims.

One Muslim leader in Detroit claimed on a radio program that there were over 600,000 Muslims in New York City alone. Such outlandish claims do their cause more harm than good.

But regardless of how many Muslims have emigrated to the West in search of employment, the host countries must try to understand and assimilate these newcomers to their shores.

Our Intent

We must state at the outset that it is not our intent in this book to offend devout Muslims. We are not trying to hurt their feelings or to embarrass them in any way.

We know from personal experience that many Muslims are good, hardworking people who have overcome impossible odds to make a new home for themselves in the West.

Freedom of Religion

Yet we also know that many Muslims take personal offense at any criticism of their religious beliefs. They find it very difficult to understand that "freedom of religion" in the West means that people are free to criticize Islam as well as any other religion! This freedom is something that we jealously guard in the West.

This is sometimes very hard for Arab Muslims to understand because they previously lived in Islamic countries, where any criticism of Muhammad or the Quran is viewed as a criminal offense punishable by death.

Under Islamic law no criticism of Islam is allowed. In other words, there is no freedom of or from religion in Muslim countries.

A Plea for Understanding

When Western scholars apply scientific standards to the truth claims of Islam, they do not want this to be construed as a personal attack on the motives or character of Muslims. The search for truth should never offend.

Indeed, an open and honest discussion of the differences between non-Muslims and Muslims can only serve to break down the walls of ignorance and prejudice.

No religion, no matter how fervently believed or zealously practiced, should be afraid of the searching light of scientific research.

The Gulf War

Once Western troops were in the Middle East, Arab dictators such as Khadafy and Saddam Hussein called for a *jihad*, or Holy War, against these soldiers. Why?

A jihad was called on the sole basis that these soldiers are, by and large, professing Christians, and thus are considered infidels according to the Islamic faith.

In other words, the dictators called upon Muslims to kill these soldiers just because they are Christians. This is a regrettable but true statement.

Religious Toleration

To the modern Western mind, religious differences should not lead to the destruction of the lives or property of anyone. People should be free to practice any or no religion according to the dictates of their own conscience.

This is why Muslims need to understand why Westerners sometimes feel uneasy about the mass migration of Arab Muslims into Europe and North America.

A Case in Point

USA Today on February 6, 1991, placed on its first two pages the result of a survey it took of Arab Muslims living in the United States concerning their attitude toward the Allied war against Saddam Hussein. The results were startling.

When asked, "Are you willing to have your son or daughter fight for the United States in this war?" 82 percent of American Arab Muslims said no.

Only 18 percent of those surveyed were willing to back America in the war against Iraq!

When asked if they approved of the way President Bush was handling the situation, 62 percent said no.

The survey went on to state that over half of American Arab Muslims said that they would *not* support a U.S. war on any Arab nation.

Why This Attitude?

For all practical purposes, this survey revealed that

many Arab Muslims have not been assimilated into the melting pot of American culture. The survey would seem to indicate that they are still more Arab than American.

The Muslim attachment to Arab culture, Arab nations, and Arab political causes even after living in the West for many years is what disturbs many Westerners.

They rightfully ask, "Just where is the allegiance of Arab Muslims? Is it to the Western nations which have given them the opportunity for a better life, or is it still only to Arab nations?"

Information Our Goal

It is our desire to inform Western people about the nature and claims of Islam and then to point out to them why Middle East scholarship has rejected those claims. We must also point out that Muslims do not hesitate to condemn and contradict the essential doctrines of other religions such as Christianity.

After visiting various Muslim information centers and mosques, I have collected a vast amount of Muslim literature which openly attacks the Bible and denies the trinity, the deity of Christ, His Sonship, His death on the cross, His bodily resurrection, and His intercession at the right hand of God the Father.[4]

Since Muslims evidently have no problem whatsoever in openly criticizing other religions, why should they have a problem with those who for good and sufficient reasons criticize Islam?

After all, the same Bill of Rights that guarantees to Muslims the freedom to criticize other religions also gives other people the freedom to criticize Islam. The sword of religious freedom always cuts both ways.

The Burden of Proof

The burden of proof for Muhammad's call to be a prophet and for the inspiration of the Quran is upon the Muslims. Thus we will be examining the arguments given by Muslims to see if in fact they hold up under careful scientific scrutiny.

One Last Note

We must point out that there are spelling variations on key Arabic words. For example, the Arabian prophet's name has been spelled Mohammed, Mohammad, Muhammed, and Muhammad. The sacred book of Islam has been spelled Coran, Koran, Qo'ran, Qu'ron, and Quran. The holy place in Mecca has been spelled Kaaba, Ka'bah, and Kabah.

In order to avoid confusion, we have adopted the spelling used in most scholarly works and journals on Islam.

A similar problem exists in the English translations of the Quran. The numbering of the verses differs from one translation to another. We will be using the numbering as given in Yusuf Ali's translation. See Appendix B at the back of this book.

PART ONE

THE NATURE
OF ISLAM

A Modern Parable

One day during a lunch break from your job in Washington D.C., you are waiting for a friend on a street corner when a strangely dressed couple approaches you and asks if they can speak to you for a moment.

The man has a powdered wig on his head and is wearing a silk shirt, a waistcoat, breeches that reach only to his knees, silk stockings, and black shoes with a silver buckle on each shoe.

The woman is wearing a powdered wig and a long, flowing dress that reaches almost to the ground. They look like a couple that has just stepped out of a movie set for an American Revolutionary War film.

The couple starts to explain to you that they are followers of a religion in which George Washington was a mighty prophet of Ba-al. Everything that George Washington taught, believed, said, and practiced must be accepted as the inspired Word of Ba-al, who is the one true God.

The speeches and letters which people think came from Washington are in the English language because that is the language of heaven. Even though there are foreign-language translations of some of these writings, they really cannot be understood unless they are read in the original English.

The speeches of Washington were actually written in heaven on a tablet of stone. George Washington did not really write a single page of his works; they were given to him by the angel Gabriel out of heaven. Washington merely recited them when Ba-al so ordered.

The strangely dressed couple went on to explain that because Washington was a prophet of Ba-al, the true God, we must live as George Washington lived. For example, all men should dress the way George Washington dressed, and all women should wear a dress such as Mrs. Washington wore.

We must even eat the food that the Washingtons ate. For example, George Washington did not like peas. Thus no one should be allowed to eat peas today.

Washington's political views must be viewed as the only valid form of government. And, since he owned slaves, slavery must be viewed as being a valid political structure for today. At that moment the alarm on the man's wristwatch goes off and he pulls a compass out of his coat pocket. After facing in a certain direction, the couple gets down on their hands and knees and bows in prayer.

After they finish their prayers, they get up. You can't help but ask them what they were doing.

They explain that they must pray five times a day toward Washington D.C. where the Washington Memorial stands. As a matter of fact, all those who are true followers of George Washington must make a pilgrimage to Washington D.C. at least once in their lifetime.

Once they get there, they must run around the Washington Memorial seven times. Then they have to run down to the end of the mall and throw some stones at the devil.

The man and his wife also remark that the Washington Memorial was actually built by Adam. Although it had been subsequently destroyed at various periods, it was eventually rebuilt by Abraham, and all the biblical patriarchs actually lived at that exact spot. The Washington Memorial is a sacred site and it has always been part of the worship of God.

At this point they ask for your opinion, so you give it: They can't really be serious about this religion of Washingtonianism. The idea of bowing in prayer toward the Washington Memorial is absurd. The memorial was not built by Adam or rebuilt by Abraham. The patriarchs did not live in Washington D.C. but in Israel. The whole thing seems ridiculous.

They respond that they are in dead earnest and that they really believe that George Washington was a prophet of Ba-al and that his writings were the Word of God.

You respond by saying, "It seems to me that you have made a religion out of eighteenth-century American colonial culture. Do you really expect people at the end of the twentieth century to live, dress, and eat in accordance with the habits and tastes of people living in the 1700's in the United States?

"What if the Russians were to invent a religion in which we were told that we had to pray toward Moscow five times a day? Why can't the Japanese invent a religion in which everyone has to pray toward Tokyo? Why can't the Mexicans say that you must take a pilgrimage to Mexico City once in your lifetime or you will not be saved?

"This whole religion seems to be silly at the least and racist at the worst. Why would you expect every culture and every race of people to live the way that people lived in eighteenth century Colonial America? It just doesn't make sense!"

At this point the man opens his coat and reveals a shoulder harness with a gun in it. He says that his religion does not allow anyone to ridicule or blaspheme the holy faith.

But at that moment, your wristwatch alarm goes off, indicating that your lunch hour is over.

With a sigh of relief you explain that you have to get back to work. But if they would like to talk with you further, they could meet you on this street corner sometime. With that said, you beat a hasty retreat without waiting for any further response from the couple.

The Key to Islam

The parable that was presented in Chapter 1 may seem farfetched, but in reality it underscores the true essence of Islam.

Western people have a difficult time comprehending Islam because they fail to understand that it is a form of cultural imperialism in which the religion and culture of seventh-century Arabia have been raised to the status of divine law.

Sacred Versus Secular

The difficulty in understanding Islam is rooted in the traditional Western philosophic concept of the secular-versus-sacred dichotomy.

In the West, organized religion is not viewed as having the power to rule over all of life; instead, there is a secular realm in which organized religion has no authority.

Thus there is a "wall of separation" between church and state. For example, religious organizations in the West cannot set speed limits or legislate political laws.

But Islam cannot be viewed simply as one's private or personal religious preference. It is not just something you believe and then go on living as you please. There is no secular realm in Islamic countries.

Seventh-Century Arabia

Islam is actually the "deification" of seventh-century Arabian culture. In a very profound sense, Islam is more cultural than it is religious.

This is why all the textbooks and the encyclopedias on Islam begin with the historical context of Muhammad and the importance of seventh-century Arabian culture.

Islam Is Arab Culture

Not too many years ago I was invited to the home of a dear black Muslim friend who lived in New York City's famous Harlem section.

When I entered his apartment I found that even though his family members were born in the United States they wore Arab clothing, listened to Arab music, and ate Arab food! They even said a blessing over the food in Arabic, although no one in the family knew the language.

They had abandoned American culture and adopted Arabian culture instead. This is what Islam meant to them.

I am not saying that Arab culture is "bad" just because it is Arab, any more than I would say that American culture is "good" just because it is American. All cultures have their good and bad points.

As a matter of fact, it was wrong for Westerners in the past to assume that their culture should be imposed upon the rest of the world. When it comes down to it,

Western cultural imperialism is as offensive as Arab cultural imperialism.

What disturbs Middle East scholars is that the Arab Muslims have gone one step further by seeking to impose seventh-century Arabian religion on *all* cultures.

Dr. Arthur Arberry

The most reliable English translation of the Quran, in our opinion, was done by Dr. Arthur J. Arberry, who was the Head of Middle Eastern Studies at Cambridge University and an outstanding professor of Arabic and Persian.

In his famous two-volume work, *Religion in the Middle East*, Prof. Arberry states that Islam is a "peculiarly Arabian religion" because Islam as a religion and a culture we recognize as fundamentally one.[1]

Even Muslim scholars such as Dr. Ali Dashti, a past Foreign Minister of Iran, in his book *23 Years: A Study of the Prophetic Career of Mohammad*, carefully documents how Islam must be understood in terms of its essential identification with seventh-century Arab culture.

Religion in the West

This connection can be hard for Westerners to understand because religion in the West is viewed as something that is intensely personal and private and not a cultural phenomenon.

For example, Christianity does not demand that people today should dress in accordance with first-century dress codes, or that they can eat only what Jesus ate. Christianity is thus "supracultural" in that it allows people to live, dress, and eat in accordance with the culture in which they are living.

But this is not so with Islam. Whenever Islam becomes the dominant religion in a country, it alters the culture of that nation and transforms it into the culture of seventh-century Arabia.

This is why it is so hard for Muslims to convert to another religion. Every aspect of life has been dictated by Islam. The Muslim must follow the dictates of Islam regardless of where he lives or what he thinks about it.

No Secular Realm

To the Muslim there is no "secular" realm where he is free from Islam. To the devout Muslim, Islam is all of life. As Kerry Lovering points out:

> Islam is a total way of life, not just a religion.[2]

In Islam there is no "separation of mosque and state" that compares to the "separation of church and state" that prevails in most Western countries. Islamic religion and politics are one. As Egyptian-born Victor Khalil points out:

> Islam regulates every aspect of life, to the point that culture, religion and politics in a Muslim country are practically inseparable.[3]

Muhammad took the Arab culture around him, with all its secular and sacred customs, and made it into the religion of Islam.

Arab Racism

Islam is fueled by a subtle form of racism in which seventh-century Arabian culture in its political expression, family affairs, dietary laws, clothing, religious rites, language, etc. is to be imposed on all other cultures.

The Ishmael Myth

One example of Arab racism is the myth that the Arabs are the descendants of Abraham through his son Ishmael. This claim was made in response to the Jews who had boasted that Abraham was the father of their race.[4]

McClintock and Strong's well-known encyclopedia on religion comments:

> There is a prevalent notion that the Arabs, both of the south and north, are descended from Ishmael; and the passage in Gen. xvi:12 ... is often cited as if it were a prediction of that national independence which, upon the whole, the Arabs have maintained more than any other people. But this supposition (in so far as the true meaning of the text quoted is concerned) is founded on a misconception of the original Hebrew.... These prophecies found their accomplishment in the fact of the sons of Ishmael being located, generally speaking, to the east of the other descendants of Abraham whether by Sara or by Keturah. But the idea of the southern Arabs being of the posterity of Ishmael is entirely without foundation, and seems to have originated in the tradition invented by Arab vanity that they, as well as the Jews, are of the seed of Abraham—a vanity which, besides disfiguring and falsifying the whole history of the patriarch and his son Ishmael, has transferred the scene of it from Palestine to Mecca.... The vast tracts of country known to us under the name of Arabia gradually

became peopled by a variety of tribes of different lineage.[5]

Most standard reference works on Islam reject the Arab claim to Abrahamic descent. The prestigious *Encyclopedia of Islam* traces the Arabs to non-Abrahamic origins.[6] Even the *Dictionary of Islam* questions the whole idea that the Arabs are descendants of Ishmael.[7]

A Radio Debate

During a radio talk show in 1991 I made the comment that the Arabs were not the descendants of Abraham. An American black Muslim called into the show to disagree with my viewpoint. He stated emphatically that the Arabs had indeed descended from Ishmael.

When I asked him for proof, all he could come up with was that he had been told by some Arab friends that this was so. Needless to say, I was not impressed by his "proof."

I then asked him, "If all the Arabs of the Middle East are the descendants of Abraham, whatever happened to all the Akkadians, Sumerians, Assyrians, Babylonians, Persians, Egyptians, Hittites, etc. that lived before, during, and after Abraham? What happened to all those millions of people who were not Abraham's descendants? Where did they go?" To this he could give no reply.

A Religious Reason

The compelling reason why Muslims claim to be descendants of Abraham is a religious one. The Quran transfers the historical setting of the biblical patriarchs from Palestine to Mecca. The Quran even has Abraham rebuilding the Kabah!

If it were admitted that Abraham never lived in Mecca and thus the Arabs are not his descendants, then the Quran itself would be overturned.

Yet the archeological evidence is overwhelming that Abraham never lived in Mecca! He came from the city of Ur, which has been found in Iraq. He then moved west to Palestine from there.[8]

The following examples will demonstrate beyond all doubt the cultural nature of Islam.

Arab Islamic Law

First, Muhammad took the political laws which governed seventh-century Arabian tribes and made them into the laws of Allah.

In such tribes the sheik, or chief, had absolute authority over those under him. There was no concept of civil or personal rights in seventh-century Arabia. The head of the tribe decided whether you lived or died.

This is why Islamic countries are always inevitably ruled by dictators or "strong men" who rule as despots. There are 21 Arab nations, and not one of them is a democracy.

Why No Democracy?

Democracy has never flourished in Arab nations because of the religion of Islam. Thus the more "secular" an Arab nation becomes, the more "democratic" it becomes. The highly secularized Egypt is an example of this phenomenon.

But whenever Islamic fundamentalism regains dominance, the nation is plunged back into the "dark ages" of seventh-century Arabia. Iran is a recent example of what happens to a nation when the Islamic clergy take over the government.

The despots of the Ottoman Empire, and the present dictators of Libya, Jordan, Iran, Iraq, Syria, Sudan, Yemen, etc. are merely examples of seventh-century Arabian tyranny transplanted into modern times.

Civil Rights

Because there was no concept of personal freedom or civil rights in the tribal life of seventh-century Arabia, Islamic law does not recognize freedom of speech, freedom of religion, freedom of assembly, or freedom of the press. This is why non-Muslims, such as Christians or Bahais, are routinely denied even the most basic civil rights.

For evidence of how Muslims have treated Jews and Christians for 1400 years, see Bat Ye'or's detailed documentation in *The Dhimmi: Jews and Christians Under Islam* (Fairleigh Dickinson University Press, 1985).

In the West, people are free to protest what their government is doing. This is why thousands of people were allowed to protest the Allied war against Iraq. They had the freedom of speech and assembly to do so.

But what if they lived in an Islamic country such as Saudi Arabia? There was no freedom to protest the war in Saudi Arabia. The Associated Press reported on February 2, 1991:

> Prince Nazef had warned that anyone undermining the kingdom's security would be executed or have a hand and a leg cut off.[9]

Those who protested the war in the West did not even get a traffic ticket, much less a leg or hand cut off!

Praying Toward Mecca

A Muslim is required to pray five times a day. This, in and of itself, is not offensive since it is good for a person to pray. However, the Muslim is told that he must pray toward Mecca, which is in Saudi Arabia, five times a day. Thus he is reminded five times a day that he must bow in obedience to Arabia.

What if there were a Russian religion that required us to bow five times toward Moscow? What about the religion of Washingtonianism which said that we must bow five times a day toward Washington D.C., or a Japanese religion that would require us to bow toward Tokyo?

The act of bowing in prayer five times a day toward Arabia is merely a symptom of the underlying cultural imperialism that lies at the heart of Islam.

Pilgrimage to Mecca

A Muslim is required, despite the hardship and great cost, to go on a pilgrimage to Saudi Arabia to worship at the Kabah in Mecca at least once in his lifetime.

Imagine if a Russian religion demanded that once in your lifetime you had to travel to Moscow and worship at Red Square, or that an American religion demanded that you had to travel to the Washington Memorial in United States.

The historical evidence is crystal clear that Muhammad adopted the pagan religious rite of a pilgrimage to Mecca to worship at the Kabah in order to appease the Meccan merchants who made a tremendous amount of money out of these pilgrimages. Thus for financial and cultural reasons Islam adopted the pagan pilgrimage to Mecca.[10]

This pilgrimage has been both cruel and unnecessary and has fostered great hardship upon poor third-world Muslims who have to skimp and save their entire life in order to fulfill this "pillar" of Islam. It makes no more sense than making a pilgrimage to Washington D.C. or Moscow.

Dietary Laws

What foods were acceptable and not acceptable in seventh-century Arabia are now mandated by Islam for all people. What Muhammad ate and did not eat is made to be a divine law for all people.

The Woman's Veil

What an illiterate, nomadic tribeswoman wore in the desert of seventh-century Arabia is mandated by Islam as the dress code for Muslim women today in every nation.

To be covered from head to foot to protect yourself from the desert sun is both practical and understandable if you are living in a desert. Arabian women dressed that way long before Muhammad was ever born. But to impose such desert garb on women everywhere is a form of cultural imperialism.

Women's Rights

The oppressive nature of Islam is seen most clearly in its denial of basic civil rights to women.

The well-known Muslim scholar Ali Dashti states:

> In pre-Islamic Arab society, the women did not have the status of independent persons, but were considered to be possessions of the men. All sorts of inhumane treatment of the women were permissible and customary.[11]

The Quran states in Sura 4:34:

Men are the managers of the affairs of women. ... Those you fear may be rebellious—admonish; banish them to their couches and beat them.

The Arabic is much stronger than the word "beat them." It actually says "scourge them." Mohammed Pickthal correctly translates it this way in his version of the Quran.

The Twig Defense

During a live phone-in radio program in Los Angeles in 1991, a Muslim claimed that the Arabic word translated "beat them" only meant "to tap lightly on the wrist with a twig."

I pointed out that the same Arabic word is used to describe the beating of camels and criminals! Who would be so foolish as to think that "tapping lightly on the wrist with a twig" could control wild camels or punish violent criminals?

Women and Islam

Dashti comments:

The statement that "men are the guardians of women" in verse 38 of Sura 4 postulates inequality of men and women in civil rights. The words are followed by two brief explanations of men's superiority over women.[12]

In Islamic law, male heirs get more than female heirs, and men's evidence is more reliable than women's; to be exact, a man's inheritance share is twice a woman's share, and his evidence carries twice the weight of hers in court.... The right to divorce belongs to the husband but not to wives.[13]

From time to time we will quote from Muslim scholars such as Ali Dashti to demonstrate that Western scholars are not operating out of a hidden bias against Islam. Their findings are supported by recognized Muslim and non-Muslim authorities in the field of Middle East studies.

The denial of civil rights to women which is clearly in the text of the Quran itself is reflective of seventh-century Arabian culture and its low view of women.

Even today, Muslim women can be kept prisoners in their own home. They can be denied the right to go outside the house if the husband so orders. They are still denied the right to vote in Islamic countries such as Kuwait!

In Islamic countries such as Iran, women must carry written permission from their husband to be out of the house! Women are even denied the right to drive a car in such places as Saudi Arabia.

A Recent Case in Point

On March 10, 1991, the *New York Times Magazine* (pp. 26-46) reported the following story on women's rights in Saudi Arabia.

> The crisis in the gulf last fall spawned a messy and much publicized demonstration by women, who dumped their chauffeurs and drove in convoy, defying an informal ban on driving by women. The incident prompted a vicious campaign against them by religious fanatics, with Government acquiescence.
>
> Underlying these strains is the question of how much power the religious establishment should have, in particular the religious police, or mutawwa. They patrol the streets and shopping malls, telling women to cover their faces and young men to pray.

The only people with spine in this society are the 47 women who drove, one Saudi intellectual said, "And look what happened to them. They were thrown to the wolves." The Government punished them as severely as it would any public protesters. Virtually all of those who taught at one university were dismissed by order of the King. The women, as well as their husbands and even some of their relatives, were forbidden to leave the kingdom.

They were ordered not to meet with Western reporters or to discuss their situation with any outsider, and they were warned of further reprisals if they attempted to drive again or stage another demonstration.

But the Government's abuse of these women was mild compared with their treatment by the religious establishment.... The fundamental sheiks denounced them from one of the kingdom's most powerful political platforms, the mosque pulpits. In Friday sermons after the protest, the women were branded as "red communists," "dirty American secularists," "whores and prostitutes," "fallen women," and "advocates of vice." Their names, occupations, addresses and phone numbers were ... distributed in leaflets around the mosque and other public places. One leaflet accused them of having renounced Islam, an offense punishable by death in Saudi Arabia.

Several of the women remained unrepentant, convinced that eventually the issue of their status will be addressed. "The issue is not driving," one of them said. "It is that here in Saudi Arabia, I exist as a person from the bellybutton to the knees."

Cruel and Unusual Punishment

Incarceration without due process; the use of torture; political assassination; the cutting off of hands, feet, ears, tongues, and heads; and the gouging out of eyes—all of these things are part of Islamic law today because they were part of seventh-century Arabian culture.[14]

To Westerners, such things are barbaric and should not have any place in the modern world.

Conclusion

Islam is a distinctively Arabian cultural religion. Unless this is firmly grasped, no real understanding of Islam is possible. Unless this fundamental point is understood, Western people will never understand why Muslims think and act the way they do.

THE CULTURAL BACKGROUND OF ISLAM

Pre-Islamic
Arabia

Since the faith of Islam deems it blasphemous to even
suggest that the teachings of Muhammad and the Quran
find their source in pre-Islamic custom, culture, and
religion, Muslims did not do any significant research on
what pre-Islamic Arabia was like.

It has been up to Western scholars since the turn of
the century to discover the cultural and literary sources
Muhammad used in the construction of his religion and
of the Quran itself. This is why every Western reference
work on Islam begins with a section on pre-Islamic
Arabia and its influence on the teachings and religious
rites of Muhammad. The historical background of Islam
cannot be ignored.

If sources for Islam can be found in pre-Islamic
Arabian culture, custom, and religion, then the doctrine
that Muhammad's faith and the Quran were brought
down from heaven and do not have any earthly human
origin would be at risk.

Circular Reasoning

Muslims frequently argue in a circle at this point. They argue that since Islam and the Quran were sent down out of heaven, no earthly sources or materials could have been used in their construction. They begin with the assumption that such things cannot be.

But Western scholarship cannot make such a gratuitous assumption. As we shall see, the Islamic faith and the Quran itself can be completely and sufficiently explained in terms of pre-Islamic Arabian culture, custom, and religion.

Special attention should be paid to the pioneering work of Julius Wellhausen, Theodor Noldeke, Joseph Halevy, Edward Glaser, William F. Albright, Frank P. Albright, Richard Bell, J. Arberry, Wendell Phillips, W. Montgomery Watt, Alfred Guillaume, and Arthur Jeffery.

Archeological and linguistic work done since the latter part of the nineteenth century has unearthed overwhelming evidence that Muhammad constructed his religion and the Quran from pre-existing material in Arabian culture. (See Appendix C.)

The Meaning of Islam

For example, the very word "islam" was not revealed from heaven or invented by Muhammad. It is an Arabic word which originally referred to an attribute of manliness and described someone who was heroic and brave in battle.

Middle East scholar Dr. M. Bravmann documents in his fascinating work, *The Spiritual Background of Early Islam*:

> [Islam was originally] a secular concept, denoting a sublime virtue in the eyes of the

primitive Arab; defiance of death, heroism;
to die in battle.[1]

The word islam did not originally mean "submission," as many people have supposed. Instead, it referred to that strength which characterized a desert warrior who, even when faced with impossible odds, would fight to the death for his tribe.

The word islam only slowly developed into meaning "submission" as Dr. Jane Smith at Harvard University has demonstrated.[2]

Pre-Islamic Tribal Life

The tribal-society aspect of pre-Islamic Arabia explains many of the things that can be found in Islam today. For example, it was perfectly in line with Arab morality to mount raids on other tribes in order to obtain wealth, wives, and slaves, and so the tribes were constantly at war with one another. But these wars did not involve a great loss of life because the weapons were quite primitive.

These desert tribes lived by the code of "an eye for an eye and a tooth for a tooth." Vengeance was extracted whenever anything was done to hurt any member of the tribe.

A harsh penal code was followed by the nomadic Arabian tribes. It meant nothing to them to cut off the right hand, a foot, or the head of someone. The tongue could be cut out, the ears lopped off, and even the eyes gouged out as punishment for various crimes.

To sneak up behind someone and slit his throat from ear to ear was viewed as the right thing to do in certain situations, and the person who did it was viewed as a hero.

Forcing people into slavery or kidnapping women, holding them in your harem, and raping them at will was considered just and proper.

The harsh Arabian climate produced a harsh tribal society in which violence was the norm. And violence is still an attribute of Islamic societies.

A Modern Example

The desperate plight of Salman Rushdie is a modern example of Arab violence.

To receive a death sentence for writing a book which gives an unfavorable view of Muhammad is something a Westerner can neither understand nor tolerate. But to an Arab Muslim, it makes perfect sense.

Dr. William Montgomery Watt of Edinburgh University has stated:

> It should be emphasized that the Arabs did not regard killing a person as in itself wrong. It was wrong if the person was a member of your kin-group or an allied group; and in Islam this meant the killing of any believer. Out of fear of retaliation one did not kill a member of a strong tribe. In other cases, however, there was no reason for not killing.[3]

In the United States, the black Muslim movement has had a particularly ugly history of violence. This violence has included assassinating their own leaders.

The Assassins

It is interesting to note that the English word "assassin" is actually an Arabic word. It comes from the Latin word *assassinus* which is taken from the Arabic word *hashshashin*.

Hashshashin literally means "smokers of hashish" and was used as a description of those Muslims who smoked hashish to whip themselves into a religious frenzy before killing their enemies.

It came into European vocabulary through the Muslim sect called "The Assassins" who believed that Allah had called them to kill people as a sacred duty.

The Assassins terrorized the Middle East from the eleventh to the thirteenth century and even made the Western explorer Marco Polo fear for his life.[4]

The Quran and Violence

This should not surprise anyone because Islam not only condones such violence but actually commands it in certain instances.

In the Quran, Muslims are told in Sura 9:5:

> Fight and slay the pagans [i.e. infidels] wherever ye find them, and seize them, beleaguer them, and lie in wait for them in every stratagem of war.

What are Muslims supposed to do to the people who resist Islam? Sura 5:33 says:

> Their punishment is . . . execution, or cruci-fixion, or the cutting off of hands and feet from the opposite sides, or exile from the land.

In the West such things as cutting off someone's hands or feet because he would not accept your religion is unthinkable.

The City of Mecca

It needs to be pointed out that Mecca was in the control of the Quraysh tribe into which Muhammad was born. Mecca was also the dominant religious center for all the pagan religions in Arabia.

Chamber's Encyclopedia points out:

> The community in which Mohammed grew up was pagan, different localities having their own gods, often represented by stones. In many places there were sanctuaries to which pilgrimage was made. Mecca contained one of the most important, the Kaaba, in which was placed the black stone, long an object of worship.[5]

Archaeologists have unearthed many examples of pre-Islamic art which includes their idols and symbols of worship.[6]

As *Encyclopedia Britannica* points out, the financial base of the Quraysh tribe depended upon the caravans and the trade routes that would particularly go through Mecca in order for pagans to worship their particular idol at the Kabah.[7]

The Kabah

The Quraysh tribe saw to it that there was an idol for every religion at the pagan temple called the Kabah. The word *Kabah* is Arabic for "cube" and refers to the square stone temple in Mecca where the idols were worshiped. The temple contained a virtual smorgasbord of deities with something for everyone.

At least 360 gods were represented at the Kabah and a new one could be added if some stranger came into town and wanted to worship his own god in addition to the ones that were already represented.

The lucrative trade routes and the rich caravans formed the cultural link between Africa, the Middle East, the East, and the West. It is therefore no surprise to find stories in the Quran whose origin can be traced back to Egypt, Babylon, Persia, India, and even to Greece.

Magic and the Genies

In terms of pre-Islamic religious life, the basic orientation of the people was that of superstition. The Arabs believed in the "evil eye," the casting of curses and spells, magic stones, fatalism, fetishes, and the fabulous stories of the jinns, or what we call in English genies or fairies.

Most people in their childhood have read some of the fantastic fables found in _The Arabian Nights_, stories of Aladdin's lamp, of flying carpets, etc.

It is no surprise therefore to find that the Quran also contains references to such things as the evil eye, curses, fatalism, and the fabulous jinns (Suras 55; 72; 113 and 114).[8]

In many Islamic countries, Muslims still wear an amulet around the neck in which a part of the Quran is recorded to ward off the "evil eye."

Animistic Religion

The Arab population was basically animistic in orientation. The male and female jinns, or spirits, existed in trees, stones, rivers, and mountains, and they were worshiped and feared.

Sacred magic stones were believed to protect the tribes. The Quraysh tribe had adopted a black stone as their tribal magic stone and had set it up at the Kabah.

This magical black stone was kissed when people came on their pilgrimage to worship at the Kabah. It was no doubt an asteroid that had fallen out of the sky and thus was viewed as being divine in some way.[9]

The Sabeans

The dominant religion that had grown very powerful just before Muhammad's time was that of the Sabeans'.

The Sabeans had an astral religion in which they worshiped the heavenly bodies. The moon was viewed as a male deity and the sun as the female deity. Together they produced other deities such as the stars. The Quran refers to this in Sura 41:37 and elsewhere.

They used a lunar calendar to regulate their religious rites. For example, a month of fasting was regulated by the phases of the moon.

The Sabean pagan rite of fasting began with the appearance of a crescent moon and did not cease until the crescent moon reappeared.[10] This would later be adopted as one of the five pillars of Islam.

Pagan Rites

Pagan ritualism also contributed to the religious world into which Muhammad was born.

The pagans of pre-Islamic Arabia taught that everyone should bow and pray toward Mecca during certain set times during the day. Everyone should also make a pilgrimage to Mecca to worship at the Kabah at least once in their life. Once they arrived at Mecca, the pagans ran around the Kabah seven times, kissed the black stone, and then ran about a mile to the Wadi Mina to throw stones at the devil.

They also believed in the giving of alms and condemned usury. They even had a certain month in which fasting was to be done according to the lunar calendar.[11]

That these pagan rites comprised the religion in which Muhammad was raised by his family is acknowledged by all. Thus it is no surprise to find that, as the Arab scholar Nazar-Ali has observed:

Islam retained many aspects of pagan religion.[12]

Alfred Guillaume, who was Head of the Depart-
ment of the Near and Middle East School of Oriental
Studies and professor of Arabic at the University of
London, and later taught at Princeton University, comments:

> The customs of heathenism have left an
> indelible mark on Islam, notably in the rites
> of the pilgrimage.[13]

Professor Augustus H. Strong has stated that Islam
"is heathenism in monotheistic form."[14]

Foreign Religions

Finally, the influence of foreign religions was also
felt in pre-Islamic Arabia.

The Jews

The Jews in large numbers had moved into Arabia
and had grown very wealthy not only in trade but also in
the gold and silver business.

Stories from the Old Testament, the Misnah, the
Talmud, and Jewish apocryphal works such as the Tes-
tament of Abraham were well known in pre-Islamic
Arabia.

The Zoroastrians

There was also the influence of the Zoroastrian
religion. Traders from Persia frequently passed through
Mecca telling their favorite fables.

Because the main trade route went through Mecca,
people from Eastern lands such as India and China also
spread their religious ideas and stories in Arabia.

It is no surprise to find that the Quran contains remnants of religious stories that can ultimately be traced back to Hinduism, Buddhism, Mythraism, Greek mystery religions, and Egyptian religions.

The Christians

Christianity had already been introduced into southern Arabia and was flourishing there by the time Muhammad was born.

But the Christianity that was present in Arabia was in an uneducated and garbled form and, worse yet, sometimes heretical in nature.

Some of the heretical teachings of the Gnostics were present in pre-Islamic Arabia in such fraudulent gospels as the Gospel of Barnabas.

These Gnostic "gospels" began to appear in the later part of the third century and reached their highest influence during the fourth through the seventh centuries. Their presence in pre-Islamic Arabia is well known.

Important Questions

The religious ideas and rites found in Islam and the Quran can be traced back to the influences of pre-Islamic culture, custom, and religious life.

Western scholars came to this conclusion when they asked the obvious question, "Why does the Quran *never* explain its ideas or rites? Why does it *never* define the meaning of such words as Allah, Islam, Mecca, jinn, pilgrimage, Kabah, etc.?"

The only rational conclusion one can come to is that the Quran does not explain such terminology because Muhammad assumed that whoever read the Quran would already be familiar with pre-Islamic culture, custom, and religious life.

This is why the Quran never explains the identity of the people mentioned in its many stories. It is assumed that the reader would already be familiar with these stories from pre-Islamic sources.

A Serious Threat

We are aware that these kinds of questions and the historical research that they generate pose a serious threat to the religion of Islam which teaches that the Quran literally came down from heaven and thus cannot have any earthly author or sources.

We understand the agony of Muslims over this issue. They are in a tight spot. To save the Quran, they must admit that Muhammad and not Allah was its author and that it was written on earth and not in heaven as it claims. This would explain all the pre-Islamic material in the Quran.

But in saving the Quran, they actually guarantee its destruction. In the end, the Muslim must give up his belief in the heavenly origin of the Quran. If this is done, Islam cannot stand.

Four

The Cult of the Moon God

By this time it should not come as a surprise that the word "Allah" was not something invented by Muhammad or revealed for the first time in the Quran.

The well-known Middle East scholar H. Gibb has pointed out that the reason that Muhammad never had to explain who Allah was in the Quran is that his listeners had already heard about Allah long before Muhammad was ever born.[1]

Dr. Arthur Jeffery, one of the foremost Western Islamic scholars in modern times and professor of Islamic and Middle East Studies at Columbia University, notes:

> The name Allah, as the Quran itself is witness, was well known in pre-Islamic Arabia. Indeed, both it and its feminine form, Allat, are found not infrequently among the theophorous names in inscriptions from North Africa.[2]

The word "Allah" comes from the compound Arabic word, **al-ilah**. *Al* is the definite article "the" and *ilah* is

47

an Arabic word for "god." It is not a foreign word. It is not even the Syriac word for God. It is pure Arabic.[3]

Neither is Allah a Hebrew or Greek word for God as found in the Bible. Allah is a purely Arabic term used in reference to an Arabian deity.

Hastings' *Encyclopedia of Religion and Ethics* states:

> "Allah" is a proper name, applicable only to their [Arabs'] peculiar God.[4]

According to the *Encyclopedia of Religion*:

> "Allah" is a pre-Islamic name ... corresponding to the Babylonian Bel.[5]

For those people who find it hard to believe that Allah was a pagan name for a peculiar pagan Arabian deity in pre-Islamic times, the following citations may be helpful:

> Allah is found ... in Arabic inscriptions prior to Islam (*Encyclopedia Britannica*).[6]

> The Arabs, before the time of Mohammed, accepted and worshipped, after a fashion, a supreme god called allah (*Encyclopedia of Islam*, ed. Houtsma).[7]

> Allah was known to the pre-Islamic Arabs; he was one of the Meccan deities (*Encyclopedia of Islam*, ed. Gibb).[8]

> *Ilah* ... appears in pre-Islamic poetry. ... By frequency of usage, *al-ilah* was contracted to *allah*, frequently attested to in pre-Islamic poetry (*Encyclopedia of Islam*, ed. Lewis).[9]

> The name Allah goes back before Muhammed (_Encyclopedia of World Mythology and Legend_).[10]

> The origin of this (Allah) goes back to pre-Muslim times. Allah is not a common name meaning "God" (or a "god"), and the Muslim must use another word or form if he wishes to indicate any other than his own peculiar deity (_Encyclopedia of Religion and Ethics_).[11]

To the testimony of the above standard reference works, we add those of such scholars as Henry Preserved Smith of Harvard University who has stated:

> Allah was already known by name to the Arabs.[12]

Dr. Kenneth Cragg, former editor of the prestigious scholarly journal _Muslim World_ and an outstanding modern Western Islamic scholar, whose works were generally published by Oxford University, comments:

> The name Allah is also evident in archeological and literary remains of pre-Islamic Arabia.[13]

Dr. W. Montgomery Watt, who was Professor of Arabic and Islamic Studies at Edinburgh University and Visiting Professor of Islamic studies at College de France, Georgetown University, and the University of Toronto, has done extensive work on the pre-Islamic concept of Allah. He concludes:

> In recent years I have become increasingly convinced that for an adequate understanding of the career of Muhammad and the

origins of Islam great importance must be attached to the existence in Mecca of belief in Allah as a "high god." In a sense this is a form of paganism, but it is so different from paganism as commonly understood that it deserves separate treatment.[14]

Caesar Farah in his book on Islam concludes his discussion of the pre-Islamic meaning of Allah by saying:

There is no reason, therefore, to accept the idea that Allah passed to the Muslims from the Christians and Jews.[15]

According to Middle East scholar E.M. Wherry, whose translation of the Quran is still used today, in pre-Islamic times Allah-worship, as well as the worship of Ba-al, were both astral religions in that they involved the worship of the sun, the moon, and the stars.[16]

Astral Religions

In Arabia, the sun god was viewed as a female goddess and the moon as the male god. As has been pointed out by many scholars such as Alfred Guilluame, the moon god was called by various names, one of which was Allah![17]

The name Allah was used as the *personal* name of the moon god, in addition to other titles that could be given to him.

Allah, the moon god, was married to the sun goddess. Together they produced three goddesses who were called "the daughters of Allah." These three goddesses were called Al-Lat, Al-Uzza, and Manat.

The daughters of Allah, along with Allah and the sun goddess were viewed as "high" gods. That is, they

were viewed as being at the top of the pantheon of
Arabian deities.

> Along with Allah, however, they worshipped
> a host of lesser gods and "daughters of Al-
> lah."[18]

The Crescent Moon Symbol

The symbol of the worship of the moon god in Arabian culture and elsewhere throughout the Middle East
was the crescent moon.

Archaeologists have dug up numerous statues and
hieroglyphic inscriptions in which a crescent moon was
seated on top of the head of the deity to symbolize the
worship of the moon god.

While the moon was generally worshiped as a female deity in the Ancient Near East, the Arabs viewed
it as a male deity.

The Gods of the Quraysh

The Quraysh tribe into which Muhammad was
born was particularly devoted to Allah, the moon god,
and especially to Allah's three daughters who were
viewed as intercessors between the people and Allah.

The worship of the three goddesses, Al-Lat, Al-
Uzza, and Manat, played a significant role in the wor-
ship at the Kabah in Mecca. The first two daughters of
Allah had names which were feminine forms of Allah.

The literal Arabic name of Muhammad's father
was Abd-Allah. His uncle's name was Obied-Allah.
These names reveal the personal devotion that Muhammad's pagan family had to the worship of Allah, the
moon god.

Praying Toward Mecca

An Allah idol was set up at the Kabah along with all the other idols. The pagans prayed toward Mecca and the Kabah because that is where their gods were stationed.

It only made sense to them to face in the direction of their god and then pray. Since the idol of their moon god, Allah, was at Mecca, they prayed toward Mecca.

The worship of the moon god extended far beyond the Allah-worship in Arabia. The entire fertile crescent was involved in the worship of the moon.

This, in part, explains the early success of Islam among Arab groups that traditionally had worshiped the moon god.

The use of the crescent moon as the symbol for Islam which is placed on the flags of Islamic nations and on the top of mosques and minarets is a throwback to the days when Allah was worshiped as the moon god in Mecca.

While this may come as a surprise to many Christians who have wrongly assumed that Allah was simply another name for the God of the Bible, educated Muslims generally understand this point.

A Muslim Taxi Driver

During one trip to Washington D.C., I got involved in a conversation with a Muslim taxi driver from Iran.

When I asked him, "Where did Islam obtain its symbol of the crescent moon?" he responded that it was an ancient pagan symbol used throughout the Middle East and that adopting this symbol had helped Muslims to convert people throughout the Middle East.

When I pointed out that the word Allah itself was used by the moon-god cult in pre-Islamic Arabia, he agreed that this was the case.

I then pointed out that the religion and the Quran of Muhammad could be explained in terms of pre-Islamic culture, customs, and religious ideas. He agreed with this!

He went on to explain that he was a university-educated Muslim who, at this point in his life, was attempting to understand Islam from a scholarly viewpoint. As a result, he had lost his faith in Islam.

The significance of the pre-Islamic source of the name Allah cannot be overestimated.

Conclusion

In the field of comparative religions, it is understood that each of the major religions of mankind has its own peculiar concept of deity. In other words, all religions do *not* worship the same God, only under different names.

The sloppy thinking that would ignore the essential differences which divide world religions is an insult to the uniqueness of world religions.

Which of the world religions holds to the Christian concept of one eternal God in three persons? When the Hindu denies the personality of God, which religions agree with this? Obviously, all men do *not* worship the same God, gods, or goddesses.

The Quran's concept of deity evolved out of the pre-Islamic pagan religion of Allah-worship. It is so uniquely Arab that it cannot be simply reduced to Jewish or Christian beliefs.

PART THREE

THE GOD OF ISLAM

Allah and the God of the Bible

Islam claims that Allah is the same God who was revealed in the Bible. This logically implies in the positive sense that the concept of God set forth in the Quran will correspond in all points to the concept of God found in the Bible.

This also implies in the negative sense that if the Bible and the Quran have differing views of God, then Islam's claim is false.

This issue can only be decided by a comparison of the two documents in question. It should not be decided on the basis of religious bias on any side but by a fair reading of the texts of both books.

The Attributes of God

The Orientalist Samuel Zwemer pointed out in 1905:

> There has been a strange neglect on the part of most writers who have described the

religion of Mohammed to study Mohammed's idea of God. It is so easy to be misled by a name or by etymologies. Nearly all writers take for granted that the God of the Koran is the same being and has like attributes as Jehovah or as the Godhead of the New Testament. Is this view correct?[1]

Most people simply assume that the God of the Bible and the God of the Quran are one and the same God, just under different names. But, as Zwemer asked, is this correct?

When we compare the attributes of God as found in the Bible with the attributes of Allah found in the Quran, it is rather obvious that these two are not the same God.

As a matter of historical record, Christian and Muslim scholars have been arguing over who has the true view of God ever since Islam arose as a religion.

The biblical view of God cannot be reduced to that of Allah any more than Allah can be reduced to the biblical God.

The historical background concerning the origin and meaning of the Arabian "Allah" reveals that Allah cannot be the God of the biblical patriarchs, the Jews, or the Christians. Allah is merely a revamped and magnified Arabian pagan moon deity.

As Dr. Samuel Schlorff points out in his article on the essential differences between the Allah of the Quran and the God of the Bible:

> I believe that the key issue is the question of the nature of God and how He relates to His creatures; Islam and Christianity are, despite formal similarities, worlds apart on that question.[2]

Let us look at some of the historic differences that have been pointed out time and again between the God

of the Bible and the Allah of the Quran. These points of
conflict have been noted in scholarly works for over a
thousand years.[3]

These points of conflict are recognized by all standard works on the subject. Therefore we will give only a
brief survey of the issues involved.

Knowable Versus Unknowable

According to the Bible, God is knowable. Jesus
Christ came into this world that we might know God
(John 17:3).

But in Islam, Allah is unknowable. He is so tran-
scendent, so exalted, that no man can ever personally
know Allah.

While according to the Bible, man can come into a
personal relationship with God, the Allah of the Quran
is so distant, so far off, so abstract, that no one can know
him.

Personal Versus Nonpersonal

The God of the Bible is spoken of as a personal
being with intellect, emotion, and will.

This is in contrast to Allah, who is not to be understood as a person. This would lower him to the level of
man.

Spiritual Versus Nonspiritual

To the Muslim, the idea that Allah is a person or a
spirit is blasphemous because this would demean the
exalted One.

But the concept that "God is a spirit" is one of the
cornerstones of the biblical nature of God as taught by
Jesus Christ himself in John 4:24.

Trinitarian Versus Unitarian

The God of the Bible is one God in three persons: the Father, the Son, and the Holy Spirit. This Trinity is not three gods but one God.

When we turn to the Quran, we find that it explicitly denies the Trinity. The Quran states that God is not a Father and Jesus is not the Son of God. Neither is the Holy Spirit God.

Limited Versus Unlimited

The biblical God is limited by His own immutable and unalterable nature. Thus God cannot do anything and everything.

In Titus 1:2, we are told, "God cannot lie." We are also told this in Hebrews 6:18. God can never act in a way that would contradict His divine nature (2 Timothy 2:13).

But when you turn to the Quran, you discover that Allah is not limited by anything. He is not even limited by his own nature. Allah can do anything, anytime, anyplace, anywhere with no limitations.

Trustworthy Versus Capricious

Because the God of the Bible is limited by His own righteous nature and there are certain things He cannot do, he is completely consistent and trustworthy.

But when we turn to study the actions of Allah in the Quran, we discover that he is totally capricious and untrustworthy. He is not bound by his nature or his word.

Love of God Versus No Love of God

The love of God is the chief attribute of the biblical God as revealed in such places as John 3:16. God has feelings for His creatures, especially man.

But when we turn to the Quran, we do not find love presented as the chief attribute of Allah. Instead, the transcendence of Allah is his chief attribute.

Neither does Allah "have feelings" toward man. That concept is foreign to Islamic teaching. That would reduce Allah to being a mere man—which again is blasphemous to a Muslim.

Active in History Versus Passive

Allah does not personally enter into human history and act as a historical agent. He always deals with the world through his word, prophets, and angels. He does not personally come down to deal with man.

How different is the biblical idea of the incarnation, in which God himself enters history and acts to bring about man's salvation.

Attributes Versus No Attributes

The Quran never tells us in a positive sense what God is like in terms of his nature or essence. The so-called 99 attributes of Allah are all negative in form, signifying what Allah is *not*, but never telling us what he *is*.

The Bible gives us both positive and negative attributes of God.

Grace Versus Works

Lastly, the Bible speaks much of the grace of God in providing a free salvation for man through a Savior who acts as an intercessor between God and man (1 Timothy 2:5).

Yet in the Quran there is no concept of the grace of

Allah. There is no savior or intercessor according to the Quran.

In conclusion, when you examine the attributes of the God who has revealed Himself in the Bible to the Allah who is described in the Quran, they are not one and the same God.

The Same God?

After presenting this material to a group of people, one person responded that he believed that Islam and Christianity worshiped the same God because they both worshiped "only one God."

What he failed to understand is that monotheism in and of itself does not tell us anything about the identity of the one God who is to be worshiped. In other words, it is not enough to say there is only one God if you have the wrong God!

Someone could say that Ra, Isis, or Osiris is the one true God, but this does not mean that Christian and Egyptian deities are one and the same.

Ancients could have taught that Ba-al or Molech was the one true God. Or again, the Greeks could have argued that Zeus or Jupiter was the one true living God.

But merely arguing that there is one God does not automatically mean that the one God you choose to worship is the right one.

In this case, the God of the Bible has revealed Himself in such a way that His nature and His names cannot be confused with the nature and names of the surrounding pagan deities.

The cult of the moon god which worshiped Allah was transformed by Muhammad into a monotheistic faith.

Because Muhammad started with a pagan god, it comes as no surprise that he ended up with a pagan god.

As the German scholar Johannes Hauri points out:

> Mohammed's monotheism was just as much
> a departure from true monotheism as the
> polytheistic ideas.... Mohammed's idea of
> God is out and out deistic.[4]

Is Allah in the Bible?

In a conversation with an ambassador from a Muslim country, I pointed out that the name Allah came from an Arabic word that had to do with the worship of the moon god in pre-Islamic Arabia. As such, it could not be found in the Hebrew Old Testament or in the Greek New Testament.

The ambassador used two arguments by which he hoped to prove that the Bible did speak of Allah.

First, he claimed that the name Allah was found in the biblical word "allelujah." The "alle" in the first part of the word was actually "Allah" according to him!

I pointed out to him that the Hebrew word *allelujah* is not a compound Hebrew word. That is, it is not made up of two words. It is one single Hebrew word which means "praise to Yahweh."[5]

Also, the name of God is in the last part of the word, *jah*, which has reference to Yahweh or Jehovah. The name Allah simply cannot be found in that word.

He then proceeded to tell me that when Jesus was on the cross and he cried out, "Eli, Eli," he was actually saying "Allah, Allah."

But this is not true either. The Greek New Testament at this point gives us the Aramaic, not the Arabic, translation of a portion of Psalm 22:1. Jesus was saying, "My God, my God, why hast Thou forsaken me?"

It is a far cry to go from "Eli, Eli" all the way to "Allah, Allah." It simply cannot be done.

Wrong Time Period

As a matter of historical record, it was impossible for the authors of the Bible to speak of Allah as God. Why?

Up until the seventh century when Muhammad made Allah into the "only" God, Allah was the name of a *pagan* deity!

Since the Bible was completed long before Muhammad was ever born, how could it speak of a post-Muhammad Allah?

In reality, the name Allah never came across the lips of the authors of Scripture.

Up until the time of Muhammad, Allah was simply one pagan god among many, his name a particular name for the moon god as worshiped in Arabia.

The biblical authors would never have confused Allah with Jehovah any more than they would have confused Ba-al with Jehovah.

The Arabic Bible

During a radio show in Irvine, California, an Arab caller responded to these observations by asking, "But doesn't the Arabic Bible use the name 'Allah' for God? Thus 'Allah' is a biblical name for God."

The answer depends on the time period. Was the Bible translated into Arabic in Muhammad's day? *No!* The first Arabic translation of the Bible did not appear until around the ninth century.

By the ninth century, Islam was the dominant political force in Arab lands and the men who translated the Bible into Arabic faced a difficult political situation. If they did not use "Allah" as the name for God, they might suffer at the hands of fanatical Muslims who, as part of their religion, believed that the Allah of the Quran was the God of the Bible.

Since "Allah" was by this time the common name for "God" because of the dominance of Islam, translators bowed to the political and religious pressures and put "Allah" into the Arabic Bible.

No Logical Bearing

Since the Arabic translation of the Bible came 900 years *after* the Bible was completed, it cannot have any bearing on whether "Allah" was originally a name for God in the Bible.

In the end, the rather obvious fact is that a ninth-century Arabic translation of the Bible cannot be used to establish the argument that the biblical authors who wrote *many* centuries earlier in Hebrew and Greek used the Arabic word "Allah" for God. Credulity has its limit!

Conclusion

Many Westerners assume that Allah is just another name for God. This is due to their ignorance of the differences between the Allah of the Quran and the God of the Bible and also due to the propaganda of Muslim evangelists who use the idea that Allah is just another name for God as an opportunity to convert Westerners to Islam.

The Bible and the Quran are two competing documents that differ in their concept of deity. This fact cannot be overlooked just because it is not in conformity with the present popularity of religious relativism.

PART FOUR

THE PROPHET OF ISLAM

The Life of Muhammad

The life of Muhammad, with all of its interesting twists and turns, can be known from the material that is found in the Quran, the Hadith, and early Muslim traditions. There are also many biographies, Muslim and Western, which have been written concerning this man.

Thankfully, the basic facts concerning Muhammad's life are well known and are not issues of controversy.[1]

Birth and Early life

Muhammad was born in A.D. 570 in Mecca to Abdullah (Abd-Allah) and Aminah. He was born into the Quraysh tribe, which was in control of the city of Mecca and which acted as the custodian of the Kabah and of the religious worship centered around it.

Even though he was distantly related to the Arab royal family of Hashim, the particular branch of the family into which Muhammad had been born was impoverished.

Muhammad's father died before he was born, and his mother died while he was still young. He was sent to live with his rich grandparents.

Muhammad's grandparents later sent him to live with a wealthy uncle, who in turn passed him on to a poor uncle who raised him as well as he could.

It is interesting to note that many of his family members never accepted Muhammad's claim to be a prophet. For example, his grandfather lived and died a pagan and never did embrace Islam.

According to the biographers and early Muslim traditions, no outstanding achievements were accomplished by Muhammad in his early life. He was a normal Arab boy who enjoyed talking with those who traveled in the caravans. He loved to explore the desert and particularly the caves. The only thing that was unusual about his childhood was that he began to experience religious visitations.

Early Visions

According to early Muslim traditions, the young pagan Muhammad experienced miraculous visions.

There is the trustworthy account in which Muhammad claimed that a heavenly being had split open his stomach, stirred his insides around, and then sewed him back up![2]

Muhammad himself later refers to this episode in Sura 94:1, which is literally translated:

Did We not open thy breast for thee?

While all the early Muslim writers, including the relatives of Muhammad, place this event in Muhammad's youth, later Muslim apologists, out of embarrassment, have tried to move it to a period after his call to be a prophet. But the historical evidence is entirely against this move.

As to the meaning of his belly being split open and his insides stirred, we are not told. But this story is so well documented that it cannot be denied.

Many Middle East scholars have felt that these early religious episodes may have been the result of some kind of mental problem or the medical problem of epilepsy.

Muhammad's Mother

Muhammad's mother, Aminah, was of an excitable nature and often claimed that she was visited by spirits, or jinns.

She also at times claimed to have visions and religious experiences. Muhammad's mother was involved in what we call today the "occult arts," and this basic orientation is thought by some scholars to have been inherited by her son.[3]

The Possibility of Epilepsy

But other scholars suggest that perhaps Muhammad's early visions were the result of a combination of epileptic seizures and an overactive imagination.

Early Muslim tradition records the fact that when Muhammad was about to receive a revelation from Allah, he would often fall down on the ground, his body would begin to jerk, his eyes would roll backward, and he would perspire profusely. They would often cover him with a blanket during such episodes.

It was while Muhammad was in such a trancelike state that he would receive divine visitations. After the trance, he would rise and proclaim what had been handed down to him.

From the description of the bodily movements that were often connected with his trances, many scholars have stated that these were epileptic seizures.

For example, the *Shorter Encyclopedia of Islam*, published by Cornell University, points out that the Hadith itself describes "the half-abnormal ecstatic condition with which he was overcome" (p. 274).

What must be remembered is that in the Arab culture of Muhammad's day, epileptic seizures were interpreted as a religious sign of either demonic possession or divine visitation.

Muhammad initially considered both options as possible interpretations of his experience. At first he worried about the possibility that he was demon possessed. This led him to attempt to commit suicide.

But his devoted wife was able to stop him from committing suicide by persuading him that he was such a good man that he could not possibly be demon possessed. More about this later.

We are aware that to even speak of the serious possibility that Muhammad may have had epileptic seizures is very offensive to Muslims. It is blasphemous for them to even consider such an interpretation.

But we would fail to convey to the reader all the facts about Muhammad if we left this out. How can we hide what many Middle East scholars have said?

Western scholars do not deny that Muhammad had experiences of some kind. But they also believe that such experiences must be interpreted and that everyone has the right to make up his own mind as to what these experiences were.

Just as Muslims are free to interpret them as divine visitations, non-Muslims are free to interpret them as epileptic seizures, demon possession, an overactive imagination, fraud, religious hysteria, or whatever gives them an adequate explanation of what Muhammad was experiencing.[4]

The reader will have to make up his own mind. Our task is to set before him all the possible options.

In McClintock and Strong's encyclopedia we read the following:

> Muhammad was endowed with a nervous constitution and a lively imagination. It was not at all unnatural for him to come after a time to regard himself as actually called of God to build up his people in a new faith.
>
> Muhammad, as we gather from the oldest and most trust-worthy narratives, was an epileptic, and as such, was considered to be possessed of evil spirits.
>
> At first, he believed the sayings, but gradually he came to the conclusion, confirmed by his friends, that demons had no power over so pure and pious a man as he was, and he conceived the idea that he was not controlled by evil spirits, but that he was visited by angels whom he, disposed to hallucinations, a vision, an audition, afflicted with the morbid state of body and mind, saw in dreams. Or even while awake, conceived he saw. What seemed to him good and true after such epileptic attacks, he esteemed revelation in which he, at least in the first stage of his pathetic course, firmly believed and which imparted to his pensive, variable character, the necessary courage and endurance to brave all mortifications and perils.[5]

Modern Reticence

We fully understand the modern reticence to point out that Muhammad's epileptic seizures could have been the source of his religious trances.

We understand that this statement will offend the sensibilities of some Muslims. But our intent is not to offend but to inform, and to establish that according to the descriptions of the physical characteristics which manifested themselves when Muhammad fell into a trance, as recorded in early Muslim traditions, we must not automatically rule out the possibility of epilepsy.

That epileptic seizures were viewed as visitations of the gods or the possession of a person by evil spirits is part of pre-Islamic Arabian superstition and religious life.

This reality, coupled with the fact that these two options were the only ones that Muhammad himself considered as possible explanations for his trances, leads one to the conclusion that he either had epilepsy or something like it.

We cannot simply ignore historical facts or seek to rewrite history in order to avoid hurting the feelings of those who do not want to hear the truth. Facts are facts regardless of how someone feels about them.

An entire generation of Islamic scholars have gone on record stating that we must consider the possibility that Muhammad was afflicted with epilepsy and that this manifested itself early on by the vision of Muhammad's belly being split open and then later by all of his "prophetic" trances.

Religious Background

As we have seen, the Quraysh tribe in which Muhammad was raised was particularly addicted to the cult of the moon god, Allah. As Muhammad grew up near the Kabah, the 360 idols, and the sacred magical black stone which was considered the "good luck charm" for the Quraysh tribe, he witnessed pilgrims coming to the Mecca every year. He watched them worship at the Kabah by running around it seven times, kissing the black stone, and then running down to a nearby Wadi to throw stones at the devil.

It is no surprise then to find that most of the elements of his religious upbringing were transferred into the religion of Islam and did not come from a "new" revelation from Allah as Islam claims.

His First Wife

Muhammad's life was uneventful as a young man. At the age of 25, he was tending a caravan. The woman who owned it was 15 years older than he was and a widow. She fell in love with him and married him. Together they had two sons, though both died young, and four daughters.

One of the daughters married Uthman, who became the caliph who later standardized the text of the Quran.

After he married the wealthy widow, Muhammad lived a life of leisure and his duties were limited to running the family produce stand in the market.

His Call to be a Prophet

At the age of 40, Muhammad experienced once again a "visitation." As a result of his religious experience, he ultimately claimed that Allah had called him to be a prophet and an apostle.

It must be pointed out that there was no tradition of being a "prophet" or "apostle" in Arabian religion.

The term "prophet" was used in the hope that the Jews would accept Muhammad as the next prophet, while the term "apostle" was likewise used in the hope that the Christians would acknowledge him as the next apostle.

Muhammad's appeal would not only be to the pagans who already joined him in worship at the Kabah in Mecca, but also to the Jews and to the Christians.

Four Conflicting Versions

In the Quran, we are told that Allah called Muhammad to be a prophet and an apostle. But, as Dr. William Montgomery Watt observed:

> Unfortunately, there are several alternative versions of these events.[6]

The Quran gives us four conflicting accounts of this original call to be a prophet. Either one of these four accounts is true and the others are false or they are all false. They cannot all be true.

In the Quran Muhammad described his initial call to be a prophet and apostle on four different occasions.

We are first told in Sura 53:2-18 and Sura 81:19-24 that Allah personally appeared to Muhammad in the form of a man and that Muhammad saw and heard him.

This is later abandoned, and we are then told in Sura 16:102 and Sura 26:192-194 that Muhammad's call was issued by "the Holy Spirit."

Since Muhammad does not really discuss who or what this "Holy Spirit" is, this is also later abandoned.

The third account of his original call is given in Sura 15:8 where we are told that "the angels" were the ones who came down to Muhammad and announced that Allah had called him to be a prophet.

Even this account is later amended in Sura 2:97, so that it is only the angel Gabriel who issues the call to Muhammad and hands down the Quran to him.

This last account of his original call was influenced by the fact that Gabriel had played a significant role in the birth both of Jesus and John the Baptist.

Some scholars believe Muhammad assumed that it was only appropriate that the next great prophet in line, being himself, should also be issued the call by Gabriel.

This fourth and last account of his initial call is the one that most Muslims and non-Muslims have heard.

Islamic Revelation

We should point out, at this point, that the concept of revelation in Islamic thought is not the same as held by Christians concerning the Bible.

The word "revelation" in Arabic literally means "handed down." It means that the Quran did not come "through" or "by" any man, Muhammad included. The Quran only came "to" man, in this case, Muhammad.

There are therefore no human authors of the Quran. Allah speaks through Gabriel to man, and man is the receiver and not the originator of the Quran.

This is in contrast to the biblical authors who even identified themselves as the ones who wrote their particular books.

Christians have no difficulty in saying Isaiah wrote the book of Isaiah or Matthew wrote the book of Matthew. They do not feel that this lessens or limits the inspiration of the Bible in any way.

But with the Quran there is the denial of any human or earthly sources for the material that was handed down from heaven by Allah through Gabriel.

Doubts and Suicide

After this initial religious experience in which he felt that he had been called to be a prophet and an apostle, Muhammad began to have grave doubts about his sanity. In particular, he was frightened that he might be demon possessed.

The bodily characteristics connected with his religious trance seemed even to Muhammad to parallel those of people in his community who would fall down in fits and of whom others would say that they were possessed of devils.

He became so depressed that he decided to commit suicide. But on his way to the place where he was going to kill himself, he fell once again into a seizure.

He experienced another vision in which he felt that he had been told not to kill himself because he was truly called of God.

Yet even after this religious experience, he still became depressed and filled with doubt.

He Begins His Preaching

When he finally opened his heart to his wife, she supported him in that she felt that God had indeed called him to be a prophet and an apostle. She encouraged him to begin to share this good news with their family and friends.

Muhammad at first shared his call only with his family and friends in secret. Indeed, his first converts were members of his own family.

Opposition Begins

But soon his message became public, and he became subject to abuse and ridicule by the population at large and even by members of his own family.

At one point the hostility against Muhammad was such that people in Mecca laid siege to the section of the city where Muhammad lived. He then faced a very difficult situation.

The Satanic Verses

In order to appease his pagan family members and the members of the Quraysh tribe, he decided that the best thing he could do was to admit that it was perfectly proper to pray to and worship the three daughters of Allah: Al-Lat, Al-Uzza, and Manat.

This led to the famous "satanic verses" in which Muhammad in a moment of weakness and supposedly under the inspiration of Satan (according to early Muslim authorities) succumbed to the temptation to appease the pagan mobs in Mecca (Sura 53:19).

The literature on the "satanic verses" is so vast that an entire volume could be written just on this one issue. Every general and Islamic reference work, Muslim or Western, deals with it as well as all the biographies of Muhammad.

The story of Muhammad's temporary appeasement of the pagans by allowing them their polytheism cannot be ignored or denied. It is a fact of history that is supported by all Middle East scholars, Western and Muslim.

We are aware that there are a few modern Muslim apologists who reject the story of the "satanic verses." But we must point out that they do so not on the basis of any historical or textual evidence. Their objection is based solely on the grounds that Muhammad was sinless and therefore could not have done this![7]

Muhammad Gets Rebuked

When his disciples at Medina heard of Muhammad's fall into polytheism, they rushed to him with rebukes and counsel.

Muhammad would later claim that Gabriel himself came down from heaven and rebuked him for allowing Satan to inspire him to concede to the Meccan worship of the daughters of Allah.

He then reverted back to his monotheism and stated that Allah can "abrogate," that is, cancel, a past revelation.

After Muhammad's death, the "satanic verses" were not included in the text of Quran. They were abrogated.[8]

This, of course, led to no end of ridicule. The pagan Meccans pointed out with glee that Muhammad's Allah simply could not make up his mind: At one point, Muhammad claimed that Allah said they could not worship the three daughters of Allah. Then Allah said that they could worship the three daughters. And now, once again, they were being told that they could not worship the three daughters. Cannot Allah make up his mind?

Forced to Flee

Because of the ridicule and the growing hostility, Muhammad left Mecca and went to Ta-if.

Finding no success or converts in Ta-if, he decided to return to Mecca.

On his way back to Mecca, according to the Quran in Suras 46:29-35; 72:1-28, Muhammad preached to and converted the jinns (genies)!

According to the Quran, the jinns in turn preached Islam to the people. Thus, the male and female spirits who inhabited the trees, the rocks, and the waters of Arabia were now Muslims and under the control of Muhammad.[9]

This is a classic form of shamanism in which Muhammad now claimed to be in control of the spirits of the earth.

Back in Mecca, he found that the hostility to his message had grown even more. The merchants in particular were deeply concerned lest the financial base of the city be destroyed by his attack on the worship of the idols that were placed at the Kabah.

Flight to Medina

Muhammad once again left Mecca and this time moved to Medina where his preaching was received.

While at Medina, Muhammad realized that his family and tribe would not give up their worship of idols unless they were forced by physical violence to do so.

The First Battle

He began to test his own power in making war by first sending out six followers who attacked a caravan, killed a man, enslaved others, and looted the caravan. This event is known as the Nakhla Raid.

All of this took place during the month which traditionally, in Arab times, was the month of truce and peace.

Muhammad received no end of criticism for violating a time of truce observed by the entire community in order to loot the caravan.[10]

The Second Battle

Now that the taste of looting and bloodshed was in the mouths of his disciples, Muhammad led the second battle himself. He and his followers won the battle of Badr.

This great success led to more followers who wanted to get in on the fighting, killing, and plundering.

Muhammad Turns on the Jews

It was at this time that Muhammad decided that the Jews were not going to convert. The Muslim scholar Ali Dashti comments:

> After the Nakhla raid, further attacks on Qorayshite caravans and unfriendly tribes met with success and helped to make the financial position of the Moslems more secure. This raiding opened the way for the acquisition of power by the Prophet Mohammad and his companions and for their eventual domination of all Arabia; but the immediate step which secured the economic

base and strengthened the prestige of the Moslems was their seizure of the property of the Jews of Yathreb.[11]

Muhammad had at first tried to encourage the Jews to accept his prophethood by preaching monotheism, observing the Jewish sabbath, praying toward Jerusalem, appealing to Abraham and the patriarchs, adopting some of their dietary laws, and praising their Scriptures.

But when it was obvious that the Jewish merchants were not going to become his disciples Muhammad decided to drop the observance of Jewish rites.

He changed the direction of prayer from Jerusalem to Mecca, dropped the Saturday sabbath and adopted the pagan Friday sabbath instead. He once again adopted the pagan religious rites in which he had been raised by his family.

But this was not all. It was at this time that Muhammad began killing Jews. At first he sent out assassins to kill individual Jews and then later on he attacked Jewish settlements.

There was a financial reason as well as a religious one for his attacks on the Jews.

Some of the Jewish settlements were centers of the gold and silver trade; by conquering such places, great wealth could be obtained quickly.

Encyclopedia Britannica points out:

> When he discovered their military incompetence he appears to have been unable to resist the temptation to appropriate their goods; and his attack on the flourishing Jewish settlement of Khaibar appears to have been designed to satisfy his discontent adherents by an accession of plunder.[12]

His First Defeat

The Meccans had finally decided that Muhammad was a serious threat and approached his band with a large army headed by Uhud.

Muhammad lost this battle although he had predicted victory. He was struck in the mouth by a sword, lost several teeth, and almost died. It was a terrible defeat for him and his followers.

Some of his followers fell away as a result of this incident. They felt they had been deceived because they had gone forth in battle expecting a glorious victory and much plunder but had to retreat in defeat with their leader and so-called prophet severely wounded.

Why the Meccans did not follow through and destroy Muhammad and his forces is not known, but after inflicting sufficient casualties to appease the sense of Arab vengeance the Meccans returned to their towns and left Muhammad in peace.

The Jewish Settlements

Muhammad then turned his attention once again to the Jews, who were easier targets than the Meccans.

He began killing the Jews and looting Jewish settlements. After one Jewish town had surrendered, 700 to 1,000 men were beheaded in one day while all the women and children were sold into slavery and the possessions of the town looted! This fact is supported by Muslim scholars as well as by Western historians.[13]

Final Triumph over Mecca

Muhammad then turned his attention again to Mecca. His forces had grown sufficiently so that he now had a large army in the field.

A treaty was established with the authorities of Mecca in which peace between Muhammad and Mecca was to last for ten years.

On the basis of the promise of peace, Muhammad and his followers would be allowed to make the pilgrimage to the Kabah and Mecca and Muhammad would be free to seek to persuade people by moral persuasion and preaching to adopt Islam, but not by force.

Within a year, Muhammad broke the treaty and with an army of thousands of followers, forced Mecca to surrender to his leadership.

Muhammad then became the undisputed political leader of Mecca as well as its undisputed religious head.

He cleansed the temple at Kabah of all its idols. He suppressed all idol worship by violence. Some of the people he had killed were ones with whom he had a personal vendetta.

For example, there was a woman poetess who had ridiculed him and had pointed out that some of the material in the Quran had actually been stolen from her poet father. She was put to death in order to silence her.

Muhammad had now achieved unbelievable success. As the undisputed head and potentate of Mecca and of its religious center, Arab tribesmen began to flock to him from all sides.

Muhammad's Personal Life

In his personal life, Muhammad had two great weaknesses. The first was greed. By looting caravans and Jewish settlements he had amassed fabulous wealth for himself, his family, and his tribe.

His next greatest weakness was women. Although in the Quran he would limit his followers to having four wives, he himself took more than four wives and concubines.

The question of the number of women with whom Muhammad was sexually involved either as wives, concubines, or devotees was made a point of contention by the Jews in Muhammad's day. Ali Dashti comments:

> All the commentaries agree that verse 57 of Sura 4 (on-Nesa) was sent down after the Jews criticized Mohammad's appetite for women, alleging that he had nothing to do except to take wives.[14]

Since polygamy was practiced in the Old Testament by such patriarchs as Abraham, the mere fact that Muhammad had more than one wife is not sufficient in and of itself to discount his claim to prophethood. But this does negate the fact that the issue has historical interest in terms of trying to understand Muhammad as a man.

It also poses a logical problem for Muslims. Because the Quran in Sura 4:3 forbids the taking of more than four wives, to have taken any more would have been sinful for Muhammad.

One Muslim apologist with whom I was conversing argued as follows:

> Muhammad was sinless. The Quran makes taking more than four wives a sin. Therefore Muhammad could not have taken more than four wives. Why? Because Muhammad was sinless.

I pointed out that the question of how many wives Muhammad or anyone else had should be answered on the basis of the historical and literary evidence and not blind faith.

Muslim scholar and statesman Ali Dashti gives the following list of the women in Muhammad's life:

1. Khadija	12. Hend
2. Sawda	13. Asma (of Saba)
3. Aesha	14. Zaynab (of Khozayma)
4. Omm Salama	15. Habla
5. Hafsa	16. Asma (of Noman)
6. Zaynab (of Jahsh)	17. Mary (the Christian)
7. Jowayriya	18. Rayhana
8. Omm Habiba	19. Omm Sharik
9. Safiya	20. Maymuna
10. Maymuna (of Hareth)	21. Zaynab (a third one)
11. Fatema	22. Khawla

Several observations need to be given about the above list:

The first 16 women were wives.

Numbers 17 and 18 were slaves or concubines.

The last four women were neither wives or slaves but devout Muslim women who "gave" themselves to satisfy Muhammad's sexual desires.

Zaynab of Jahsh was originally Muhammad's adopted son's wife. The fact that Muhammad took her for himself has been problematic to many people, Muslims included.

Aesha was only eight or nine years old when Muhammad took her to his bed. This facet of Muhammad's sexual appetite is particularly distressing to Westerners.

While in Islamic countries an eight- or nine-year-old girl can be given in marriage to an adult male, in the West, most people would shudder to think of an eight- or nine-year-old girl being given in marriage to anyone.

This aspect of Muhammad's personal life is something that many scholars pass over once again because they do not want to hurt the feelings of Muslims. Yet, history cannot be rewritten to avoid confronting the facts that Muhammad had unnatural desires for little girls.

Finally, Mary, the Coptic Christian, refused to marry Muhammad because she would not renounce Christianity and embrace Islam. She bravely chose to remain a slave rather than convert.

The documentation for all the women in Muhammad's harem is so vast and has been presented so many times by able scholars that only those who use circular reasoning can object to it.

Muhammad's Death

As to the circumstances of Muhammad's death in A.D. 632, there is some confusion.

The traditional view is that his death was due to poisoning by a Jewish woman whose relatives were murdered in one of Muhammad's pogroms against the Jews.

Yet because this poisoning incident may have taken place one to two years before his death, it seems hard to believe that the poison did not kill him until that time.

It is also apparent from the early biographers that Muhammad had no premonition of his own death. He had made no arrangements for a successor. He did not set up any kind of governmental bureaucracy to run things in the event of his death.

Neither did he gather or put together his various revelations into what is now known as the Quran. His death was sudden and gave him no time whatever to arrange his own affairs.

Because Muhammad had not clearly spelled out what was to be done after his death, Islam soon broke into warring sects such as the Shiites and the Sunnis.

Conclusion

The amazing genius and forceful personality of Muhammad enabled him to take a minor pagan cult of the worship of the moon god Allah and to turn it into the second-largest religion in the world!

Seven

Muhammad and Jesus Christ

Since Islam claims that Muhammad and Jesus of Nazareth were both Muslims and both prophets sent by Allah, these two mighty prophets must coincide in all points and never contradict each other.

After all, if the same Allah sent both of them, it is only logical to assume that their ministries and messages cannot in principle contradict each other. Otherwise, Allah would be contradicting himself!

This is, of course, received as a tenet of faith by the orthodox Muslims and is not open to question in their minds.

Yet Westerners cannot gratuitously accept such a belief without first comparing the ministries and messages of these men to see if, in fact, they are in complete accord.

How to Do It

But how is this to be done? Everyone agrees that the life and teaching of Muhammad can be reconstructed from the Quran. But what about Jesus of Nazareth?

Some Muslims attempt to block any attempt to compare the biblical Jesus to the quranic Muhammad by claiming that the Bible is hopelessly corrupt and that the Jesus of the New Testament is not the true Jesus.

But this approach lands them in yet deeper problems. Because the Quran uses the New Testament Gospels for information on Jesus (such as His virgin birth), if they are corrupt, then so is the Quran.

Modern Muslim attempts to limit our information about Jesus to what the Quran says about Him once again reflect circular reasoning.

In one friendly debate with a Muslim student, the following conversation took place:

> Muslim: The Quran is true in all things.
>
> Non-Muslim: But it contradicts the biblical Jesus.
>
> Muslim: Then the Bible is corrupt.
>
> Non-Muslim: But how do you know that the Bible is "corrupt"? Do you have any textual proof?
>
> Muslim: I don't need any textual proof because I know that the Bible is corrupt.
>
> Non-Muslim: But how do you know this?
>
> Muslim: The Quran is true in all things.

A Different Approach

Perhaps the best way to deal with this issue is to lay aside all *a priori* assumptions of the inspiration of either the Bible or the Quran and simply compare the Bible and the Quran as two literary documents.

This literary approach will help us stay objective in comparing the life of Jesus and the life of Muhammad.

Founding Documents Only

In this literary comparison, we will restrict ourselves to the founding literary documents of each religion.

The life of Muhammad will be drawn only from the Quran just as the life of Jesus will be drawn only from the New Testament. This will keep things honest and fair.

We will not utilize any of the later Muslim legends which try desperately to elevate Muhammad's life above mediocrity and add to it elements of the miraculous.

Due to the limitations of this book, we can give only a brief survey of a number of the comparisons between Muhammad and Jesus.

Those readers who wish to study this issue in depth should consult Alfred Guillaume's book, *The Traditions of Islam*, which is the fullest treatment we know on the subject.

Prophecy

First, the birth, life, death, and resurrection of Jesus were clearly prophesied in the Old Testament according to the New Testament.

Several examples will suffice. Micah 5:2 gives us the very name of the town in which the Messiah would be born. On the day Christ died, no less than 33 Old Testament prophecies were fulfilled. The coming of Christ was preceded by the preaching of John the Baptist, in the spirit and power of Elijah, according to the prophecy in Isaiah 40 and Malachi 4.

This is in stark contrast to the coming of Muhammad, which was not predicted by pagan soothsayers, Old Testament prophets, or New Testament apostles.

That this point is well taken is proved by the extreme lengths some Muslims will go to in trying to manufacture some biblical prophecies for the coming of Muhammad.

Some of these claims are so outlandish that they need only be noted to refute them.

For example, one American black Muslim tried to convince me that the word "amen" in the Bible actually meant "Ahmend" that is, Muhammad!

The vain attempt of some modern Muslims to claim that when Jesus predicted the coming of a comforter in John chapters 14, 15, and 16, He was referring to Muhammad, falls to the ground when one reads John 14:26 where the comforter is specifically identified as the Holy Spirit whom the Father will send in the name of Jesus Christ.

Other biblical passages have been cited by Muslim apologists from time to time but without any concern for the original language or the context of the text. They have been ably dealt with by Western scholars.[1]

Muhammad never claimed to be the Holy Spirit who had come in the name of Jesus Christ. Thus we find that while the coming of Christ was preceded by numerous prophecies the coming of Muhammad was not predicted by anyone.

Births

The birth of Jesus Christ was miraculous in that He was conceived by the Holy Spirit in the womb of the virgin Mary.

The Quran and orthodox Islam fully accept the virgin birth of Jesus. It is only in modern times that we find some small heretical Muslim groups who deny and ridicule the doctrine of the virgin birth of Jesus.

They do this out of a reaction to the fact that there was nothing miraculous or supernatural about the birth of Muhammad. He was the natural product of the sexual union of his father and mother.

Sinlessness

According to the New Testament, Jesus Christ lived a perfect and sinless life (2 Corinthians 5:21).

When His enemies came to accuse Jesus before Pilate and Herod, they had to invent charges because no one could find anything against Him.

But when we turn to the life of Muhammad, we find that he was a normal human being engaged in the same sins which afflict all of us. He lied; he cheated; he lusted; he failed to keep his word, etc. He was neither perfect nor sinless.

A Sinful Muhammad?

After I had given a lecture on Islam at the University of Texas (Austin) in 1991, I was challenged by some Muslim students to prove that Muhammad was a sinner.

My first response was to point out that the burden of proof was not on me but on them. I then asked, "Where in the Quran is it ever stated that Muhammad was sinless?"

They could not refer me to a single passage in which such an idea is even suggested, much less taught.

They demanded that I show from the Quran where Muhammad was said to be a sinner. I answered their challenge by citing several passages from the Quran which clearly reveal to any honest reader that Muhammad was a sinner.

The Quranic Muhammad

In Sura 18:110, and elsewhere, Muhammad is commanded by Allah:

Say, I am but a man like yourselves.

Nowhere in the Quran is Muhammad said to be sinless. Instead, Allah tells Muhammad that he is no different than any other man.

Those Muslims who claim that Muhammad was sinless have failed to note Sura 40:55, where Allah told Muhammad to repent of his sins!

Muhammed Pickthal translates Sura 40:55 as saying:

Ask forgiveness of thy sin.

The only way out of this passage is to state that Allah was wrong to ask Muhammad to ask for forgiveness because he had nothing to forgive!

Pickthal's translation of Sura 48:1,2 states:

Lo! We have given thee,
    (O Muhammad) signal victory,
that Allah may forgive thee
of thy sin, that which is
past and that which is to
come, and may perfect His
favour unto thee, and guide
thee on a right path.

Not only was Muhammad commanded to repent of his sins and to seek forgiveness, but he was also reminded of his past sins that Allah had already forgiven and of future sins which would need future forgiveness!

Muhammad was not sinless according to the Quran. He was just one more poor sinner in need of forgiveness and redemption.

Miracles

During his lifetime, Jesus did many great and mighty miracles. He healed the sick, raised the dead, cast out demons, and even ruled the wind and the waves.

But according to the Quran in dozens of places such as Sura 17:91-95, Muhammad never performed a single miracle.

The only sign that Muhammad could point to was the existence of his revelations, the Suras, that made up the Quran (Sura 29:47-51).

Alfred Guillaume points out:

> Controversy with Christians on the rival merits of Jesus and Muhammad may fairly be regarded as the origin of the pretended miracles, flatly contradicting the plain statement of the great Arabian and those of many of his immediate followers that he was not sent with power to work miracles. Whether the object of the inventors was to elevate their prophet to a position equal to that held by Jesus in the estimation of His servants, or whether it was to furnish themselves and their pupils with a messenger of God who satisfied a natural craving of the human heart for a visible manifestation of divine power it is not our purpose to determine. There are good reasons for believing that deliberate imitation was resorted to for the reasons already given, and because the *ashabu-l-hadith* did not stop at ascribing the works of Christ to their prophet. His words and those of his apostles are freely drawn on and put into the mouth of Muhammad.[2]

Muhammad did no miracles. He did not heal the sick, raise the dead, cast out demons, or rule the wind and the waves. He had no more power than any normal man.

Ali Dashti comments:

Moslems, as well as others, have disregarded the historical facts. They have continually striven to turn this man [Muhammad] into an imaginary superhuman being, a sort of God in human clothes, and have generally ignored the ample evidence of his humanity. They have been ready...to present these fantasies as miracles.[3]

Many Iranians have been raised on a diet of myth and are ready to believe that any *emamzada*, of however ancestry, can at any moment perform a miracle. But if they were to read the Qor'an, they would be surprised to find no report of a miracle in it at all. They would learn from twenty or more Qor'anic passages that whenever the Prophet Mohammad was asked by doubters to perform a miracle, he either stayed silent or said that he would not do so because he was a human being like any other, with no function except to communicate, to be a "bringer of good news and a warner."[4]

The Love of God

According to the New Testament, Jesus preached the love of God and was the greatest example of that love:

God so loved the world, that He gave His only begotten Son, that whoever believes in Him should not perish but have eternal life (John 3:16).

In contrast, we do not have any record in the Quran of Muhammad ever preaching the love of God.

As a matter of fact, neither God's love for man nor man's love for God plays any significant role in the preaching of Muhammad, the Quran, or the religion of Islam.

Whereas Christianity can point to the coming of Christ as the greatest proof and example that God loves mankind, Islam cannot point to anything that reveals the love of God.

Human and Divine Nature

According to the New Testament Jesus Christ was unique in that He was divine as well as human. This is why Jesus is called "God" in John 1:1,18; 20:28; Acts 20:28; Romans 9:5; Titus 2:13, Hebrews 1:8, 10; 2 Peter 1:1, etc.

When we turn to Muhammad, we find that he was only a man.

On Beauty of Speech

When you study the speeches of Jesus as given in the Gospels, for example, the Sermon on the Mount, you find that Jesus was the greatest speaker who ever lived.

Even His enemies had to confess that no man ever spoke as He spoke.

But when you turn to the ecstatic, confused speeches of Muhammad as found in the Quran, you do not find anything outstanding. There is nothing which matches the beauty, substance, or style of the way that Jesus preached the gospel during His lifetime.

A High Moral Example

The way Jesus lived and the way He was willing to die for sinners has given us a high moral example to follow.

But when you turn to the example of Muhammad, you do not find a high moral example; you find him involved in many acts which must be deemed as immoral and unjust.

Killing or Robbing

Jesus never killed or robbed anyone. If He had done so, this surely would have been brought up during His trial.

When we turn and look at the life of Muhammad we find that he clearly killed and robbed people in the name of Allah according to the Quran.

Coercion

Jesus never used physical violence to force people to believe His message or to accept Him as the Messiah.

As a matter of fact, when Peter took out his sword Jesus told him to put it back in its sheath, that physical persuasion through violence was not the way of His kingdom (Matthew 26:51-54).

But when we turn to the example of Muhammad, we find that he frequently used physical violence to force people to give up their idols and to accept Islam.

Directing Disciples to Kill

Jesus never instructed His followers by way of command, example, or precept to kill in His name, to rob in His name, or to subdue enemies in His name.

But Muhammad did. He taught his disciples by example, command, and precept that they could and should kill and rob in Allah's name and force people to submit to Islam.

On Taking Another Man's Wife

Jesus did not take any man's wife to be his wife.

But Muhammad did. This is one of the most distressing aspects of Muhammad's life.

Muhammad's adopted son, Zaid, had married a beautiful young woman with whom he was deeply in love.

Then one day, according to early Muslim traditions, Muhammad saw Zaid's wife without her veil. Her beauty was such that he lusted after her.

He asked Zaid to divorce his wife and to give her to him. But Zaid and his wife refused such an outrageous request.

Faced with the refusal of Zaid and his wife to dissolve their marriage, Muhammad had a "convenient" revelation from Allah, which not only commanded Zaid to give up his wife to Muhammad but also decreed that there was no evil in a father-in-law taking his daughter-in-law away from his own adopted son!

Zaid and his wife were told that they did not have any choice in the matter. They had to submit to the will of Allah.

> It is not for any believer, man or woman, when God and His Messenger have decreed a matter, to have the choice in the affair. Whosoever disobeys Allah and His Messenger has gone astray into manifest error. When you said to him whom Allah had blessed and you had favoured, "Keep your wife to yourself, and fear Allah," and you were concealing within yourself what Allah should reveal, fearing other men; and Allah has better right for you to fear him. So when Zaid had accomplished what he would of her, then We gave her in marriage to you, so that there should not be any fault in the believers, touching the wives of their adopted sons, when they have accomplished

what they would of them; and Allah's com-
mandment must be performed. There is no
fault in the prophet, touching what Allah
had ordained for him (Sura 33:36-38).

It is no wonder that this passage in the Quran has
led many Muslims to renounce Islam.

Child Brides

Jesus was never a child molester or someone who
was sexually involved with young children.

But this is the only description that one can give of
Muhammad's marriage to an eight-year-old girl who
was still playing with her dolls according to the Hadith.

Unclean Foods

Jesus released his followers from all Jewish dietary
laws and in so doing made all foods clean (Mark 7:14-23).

Muhammad, on the other hand, maintained the
dietary laws of his day, and so his followers are forbidden
to eat pork or drink wine.

On Dying for Others

When Jesus Christ died, He died for the sins of His
people in order to deliver them from the wrath of God
(1 Corinthians 15:3,4).

But when Muhammad died, he died for his own
sins. He did not die for anyone.

Resurrection

Jesus did not remain dead. He conquered sin, hell,
and the grave, and physically rose again on the third

day in the same body that had hung on the cross. Just as He died for our sins, He arose again according to the Scriptures for our justification (Romans 4:25).

But when Muhammad died, he stayed dead. He did not rise from the dead. Muhammad is dead while Jesus Christ is alive.

Ascension

Jesus ascended bodily into heaven. This was witnessed by the disciples in Acts 1:9-11.

But Muhammad did not ascend into heaven. The Quran never states that he ascended.

Heavenly Intercession

Jesus is now in heaven as our intercessor and Savior, the only mediator between God and man (1 Timothy 2:5).

But Muhammad is not an intercessor or a savior. In fact the Quran states that there is no intercessor or savior (Sura 6:51,70;10:3). You have to save yourself.

Worship

In the New Testament, Jesus was worshiped as a living Savior (John 20:28).

But the Quran never speaks of worshiping Muhammad. That would be blasphemous.

Muslims will admit that Muhammad should not be worshiped by anyone because he was only a man.

Personal Relationship

According to the New Testament people can have a personal relationship with Jesus Christ as He enters into their hearts through His Spirit at conversion. This is why Christians talk about their love of Jesus.

On the other hand, what Muslim speaks of Muhammad in terms of loving him? There is no personal relationship possible with Muhammad. He is dead!

Returning to Earth

Jesus will return to resurrect and judge all men. Even orthodox Muslims will often admit that this is clearly true.

But at the same time it must be stated that there is no teaching in the Quran that says that Muhammad will return one day or that he will resurrect or judge anyone.

In Search of the Historical Muhammad

Now to be sure, Western scholars are perfectly aware of the fact that in later conflicts between Muslims and Christians there were those Muslims who attempted to renovate the life of Muhammad so that it would more closely correspond to the life of Jesus Christ.

According to Ali Dashti, these stories are "an example of myth-making and history-fabrication of Moslems."[5]

These later legends claim predictions were made for Muhammad's coming, add a supernatural element to his birth, depict him doing miracles, and claim that he was sinless and perfect and that he ascended into heaven. But these claims are not found in the Quran or in early Muslim traditions.

As all the standard reference works point out, they are later fabrications made by embarrassed Muslims who were faced with the rather obvious fact that

Muhammad was inferior to Jesus Christ. This led them to remold the life of Muhammad to parallel the life and miracles of Jesus. As Professor Guillaume observes:

> Muslim theologians... borrowed also events from the life of Jesus, attributing them to their prophet.[6]

> Muhammadan apologists could not afford to allow their apostle to labour under the disadvantage apparent when his everyday mundane life was compared with the mighty works of Christ.... The curious and interesting fact is that the later picture of Muhammad approximates... that of the Jesus of the Gospels.[7]

A Hindu Parallel

We are reminded of the followers of Krishna in India who, in response to the Christian teaching that Jesus died on the cross for our sins, immediately answered, "Well, then Krishna too must have died on a cross for our sins."

This fabrication did not last long as it was revealed that in all the literary sources concerning Krishna, no such death or crucifixion was mentioned until *after* the followers of Krishna had engaged in debate with Christians.

In the same way, Muslim legendary material concerning the miracles of Muhammad all date *after* heated debates between Christians and Muslims.

These myths and legends were created in response to the challenge that Jesus Christ was obviously superior to Muhammad.

Conclusion

Anyone who rationally examines the differences between the biblical Jesus and the quranic Muhammad must come to the conclusion that Jesus and Muhammad did not both represent the same God. They did not live or preach like each other. On all the essential issues they were poles apart.

PART FIVE

THE SACRED BOOK OF ISLAM

The Structure of the Quran

When a person who is familiar with the Bible picks up a Quran and begins to read it, he immediately recognizes that he is dealing with an entirely different kind of literature than that which is found in the Bible. Whereas the Bible contains much historical narrative, the Quran contains very little. Whereas the Bible goes out of its way to explain unfamiliar terminology or territory, the Quran does not.

Structural Differences

In fact, the very way that the Bible is structured, as a library of 66 books, reveals that it is ordered according to chronology, subject, and theme.

But when you turn to the Quran, you find a jumbled and confused ordering of individual Suras.

Some Western scholars have stated that the structure of the Quran is so mixed up that it requires the utmost sense of duty for anyone to plow through it!

107

Western Comments

The Scottish scholar Thomas Carlyle once said:

> It is a toilsome reading as I ever undertook,
> a wearisome, confused jumble, crude, incon-
> dite. Nothing but a sense of duty could carry
> any European through the Koran.[1]

The German scholar Salomon Reinach has stated:

> From the literary point of view, the Koran
> has little merit. Declamation, repetition,
> puerility, a lack of logic and coherence strike
> the unprepared reader at every turn. It is
> humiliating to the human intellect to think
> that this mediocre literature has been the
> subject of innumerable commentaries, and
> that millions of men are still wasting time
> in absorbing it.[2]

Historian Edward Gibbon has described the Quran as "an incoherent rhapsody of fable, and precept, and declamation, which sometimes crawls in the dust, and sometimes is lost in the clouds."[3]

McClintock and Strong's encyclopedia concludes:

> The matter of the Koran is exceedingly
> incoherent and sententious, the book evi-
> dently being without any logical order of
> thought either as a whole or in its parts.
> This agrees with the desultory and inciden-
> tal manner in which it is said to have been
> delivered.[4]

Even the Muslim scholar Ali Dashti laments the literary defects of the Quran:

Unfortunately the Qor'an was badly edited and its contents are very obtusely arranged. All students of the Qor'an wonder why the editors did not use the natural and logical method of ordering by date of revelation, as in 'Ali b. Abi Taleb's lost copy of the text.[5]

The standard Islamic reference work, *The Concise Encyclopedia of Islam*, refers to the "disjointed and irregular character" of the text of the Quran.[6]

To find literary parallels to the Quran, one must search into the pre-Islamic Arabic literature where we find numerous examples of such ecstatic and often confused poetic material.

Mecca and Medina

Muhammad's religious ministry as contained in the Quran was spread over two different periods. The first one took place in Mecca beginning at least by the year A.D. 612 and lasting approximately ten years.

The other period is centered in Medina and once again lasts approximately ten years until Muhammad's death in A.D. 632.

This twofold division of Meccan ministry and Medinan ministry has been acknowledged by most scholars in the field.

An Unforeseen Death

As we have already pointed out, Muhammad did not foresee his own death, although he claimed to be a prophet of God. Therefore he made no preparations for the gathering together of his revelations so that they could be placed into one document.

No Original Manuscripts

From historical accounts that are unimpeachably accurate and trustworthy, we know that when Muhammad fell into his seizures or trances and then spoke to others what he saw during such episodes, he did not write these things down on a manuscript.

Despite the farfetched claims of some modern Muslim apologists, Muhammad himself did not write or prepare the final manuscript of the Quran.

His death was unexpected, not only by his followers, but also by him. He did not even have the opportunity to gather together the scattered records of some of his Suras.

Bones, Leaves, and Stones

It was left up to Muhammad's followers to try and write down what he said. These records were written on whatever was handy when Muhammad fell into one of his unpredictable trances.

The *Concise Encyclopedia of Islam* comments:

> The Koran was collected from the chance surfaces on which it had been inscribed: "from pieces of papyrus, flat stones, palm leaves, shoulder blades and ribs of animals, pieces of leather, wooden boards, and the hearts of men."[7]

Even the internationally known Muslim scholar Mandudi admits that the Quran was originally recorded "on leaves of date-palms, barks of trees, bones, etc."[8]

The strange materials on which the Quran was written are verified by all general reference works such as the encyclopedias and by the standard reference works on Islam.

When there was nothing around which could be written on, the attempt was made to memorize Muhammad's revelations as closely as possible.

According to Mandudi, the task that confronted the followers of Muhammad after his unexpected demise was to gather together the scattered sermons of Muhammad, some of which were written on biodegradable articles, and others which were not written down but committed only to memory.[9]

This, of course, created great difficulties. Some of the tree bark crumbled or broke and some of the stones were lost. Worse yet, Ali Dashti notes that animals at times ate the palm leaves or mats on which the Suras had been recorded.[10]

Some of those who were the only ones who remembered certain Suras died in battle before they had the opportunity to commit in writing what they had heard.

The gathering together of Quranic material lasted for several years. Much confusion reigned as the memory of one person would not exactly correspond to the memory of another.

This is a sad fact of the human nature that cannot be overlooked. When more than one person is present and hears the same speech, disagreement as to exactly what was said can often arise.

As we shall see later on, this was overcome by the use of physical force and the attempt to coerce people to use one particular version of what Muhammad said as opposed to other versions.

The Order of the Suras

As you pick up the Quran, you will discover that the 114 Suras, or revelations, given to Muhammad are not laid out in the chronological order in which Muhammad received them.

If this were so, then the first Sura would be the first revelation Muhammad received and the last Sura would be the last revelation.

Neither is the Quran laid out in terms of a progressive historical narrative in which we follow the life, actions, and teachings of Muhammad from beginning to end.

We are confronted instead with a jumbled mass of Suras which defy any natural organization according to context.

The way that the Quran was put together by those left behind after Muhammad died was to simply do so on the basis of size.

Thus the Quran is arranged from the biggest Sura down to the smallest Sura, irrespective of the chronology in which an individual Sura was given.

Mass Confusion

This causes tremendous problems and confusion. In the Quran one will often find that what is clearly commanded in the first part of the Quran is "abrogated," that is, contradicted, by something that is written in the latter part of the Quran.

To reconstruct the life and teaching of Muhammad in a chronological order, one must jump all over the Quran from one Sura to another.

This, of course, causes tremendous confusion to anyone who attempts to understand the Quran as a piece of literature.

Dating the Suras

Since religious leaders tend to get long-winded the longer they minister, most scholars believe that the shortest Suras are the first ones Muhammad preached.

As time went on, the Suras got longer as he had more to say.

But there is at times a mixture of Meccan and Medinan revelations in the same Sura so that even size is not an infallible guide in dating the Suras.

First Person

Muslims claim that the Quran is always written in the first person, that Allah himself is always speaking to man.

Such a claim, however, does not fit the text of the Quran. There are many sections in which it is clear that Allah is *not* speaking, but Muhammad *is*.

Endless Repetition

Another problem with the Quran is that since it was intended to be memorized by those who were illiterate and uneducated, it engages in endless repetition of the same material.

One frequently encounters the same stories over and over again in the Quran.

While this is no doubt helpful to the illiterate masses often found in the Muslim world, it does make it more tedious for literate people.

The Right "Feel"

The last observation about the Quran as a whole is that it does not have the feeling that it is complete.

When you pick up the Bible, you find that it begins at the *beginning* of all things, the creation of the heavens and the earth (Genesis 1:1).

As you proceed through the Bible, you learn in chronological order about creation, the fall of man into sin, the great flood, the tower of Babel, the calling of Abraham, the patriarchs, the calling of Moses, the exodus, the building up of the nation of Israel, the ultimate captivity of the nation, the people going into exile, their return under Cyrus, the rebuilding of Israel, the prediction of the coming of the Messiah, the coming of the Messiah and His life, death, and resurrection, and the beginning of the church age. Then you come to the last book of the Bible, and you read about the *end* of the universe.

The Bible gives us a sense of wholeness or completeness for it begins at the *beginning* and runs all the way through to the *end* of history.

No Beginning or End

But when you turn to the Quran, because of its disordered condition, you are not left with that feeling of completeness.

You are, as it were, left hanging after each Sura because there is no logical connection from one to the other.

For example, one Sura will deal with some pedestrian matter such as Allah wanting Muhammad's wives to stop arguing and bickering in his presence while the next Sura attacks the idols of the Arabians.

Thus you are left with a feeling of incompleteness and dissatisfaction that you are not getting the whole story.

Conclusion

If you were to contrast the 66 books of the Bible written over a period of several thousand years by at least 40 different authors with the Quran which came through one man, Muhammad, during his lifetime, there would be no contest as to which was the superior literature.

The fact that the Quran claims that it is a continuation of the Old and New Testaments is actually damaging to the Muslim cause because the Quran, in the final analysis, simply does not fit the literary style or structure that is found in the Old and New Testaments.

Most Western scholars have concluded that to go from the Bible to the Quran is to go from the superior to the inferior, from the greater to the lesser, from the real to the counterfeit.

Muslim Claims for the Quran

The claims that Muslims make for the origin, history, composition, and preservation of the text of the Quran are so startling that they must be examined in more detail.

Perfect Arabic

Muslims claim that the text of the Quran is written in perfect Arabic in every respect because Allah wrote it in heaven.

The *Shorter Encyclopedia of Islam* states:

> To Muslims the absolute perfection of the language of the Koran is an impregnable dogma.[1]

Since whatever Allah does must be perfect, the Quran must be in perfect Arabic. This claim is found in Suras 12:2; 13:37; 41:41,44.

A Table in Heaven

Muslims believe Allah wrote the Quran in heaven on a stone tablet the size of a table before it was handed down to Muhammad.

No Variant Readings

It is further claimed that because the Quran is perfect, there are no variant readings, lost verses, or conflicting manuscripts on the text of the Quran.

At this point, Muslim apologists have pointed out that while the Bible has many conflicting readings on various texts, the Quran is perfect and thus has no variant readings.

The Originals Found

Many Muslims have told us with absolute confidence that the "original manuscript" of the Quran which Muhammad himself gathered and constructed is still in existence and all Qurans come from this one single original manuscript.

No Translations

Because the Quran is in the language of Allah, Muslims claim that no mortal man can translate it into another language.

Nothing to Compare

According to Muslims, no one can write any literature like that found in the Quran (Sura 10:37,38).

Are These Things So?

Are these claims true? Are they in accord with the

facts? We have to state, quite unequivocally, that these claims are false.

Not Perfect Arabic

First of all, the Quran is not in perfect Arabic. It contains many grammatical errors, such as in Suras 2:177,192; 3:59; 4:162; 5:69; 7:160; 13:28; 20:66; 63:10, etc.

Ali Dashti comments:

> The Qor'an contains sentences which are incomplete and not fully intelligible without the aid of commentaries; foreign words, unfamiliar Arabic words, and words used with other than the normal meaning; adjectives and verbs inflected without observance of the concords of gender and number; illogically and ungrammatically applied pronouns which sometimes have no referent; and predicates which in rhymed passages are often remote from the subjects.[2]
>
> To sum up, more than one hundred Qor'anic aberrations from the normal rules and structure of Arabic have been noted.[3]

Foreign Words

In addition there are parts of the Quran that are not even in the Arabic language!

In his book, *The Foreign Vocabulary of the Quran*, Arthur Jeffery documents the fact that the Quran contains over 100 foreign (non-Arabic) words.[4]

There are Egyptian, Hebrew, Greek, Syriac, Akkadian, Ethiopian, and Persian words and phrases in the Quran.

Middle East scholar Canon Sell observes:

> The number of foreign words is very great. They are borrowed from many languages. In the *Mutawakkil* by Jalalu's-Din as-Syuti one hundred and seven words are enumerated and commented on.
>
> This valuable book has been translated by W.Y. Bell, Yale University. The Arabic text is also given. It incidentally shows how many ideas have been borrowed.[5]

Many Variant Readings

Muslims attack the Bible on the grounds that it sometimes has conflicting wording from different manuscripts. Yet this is exactly the case with the text of the Quran. There are many conflicting readings on the text of the Quran as Arthur Jeffery has demonstrated in his book, *Material for the History of the Text of the Quran.*[6]

At one point, Jeffery gives 90 pages of variant readings on the text. For example, in Sura 2 there are over 140 conflicting and variant readings on the text of the Quran.

All Western and Muslim scholars admit the presence of variant readings in the text of the Quran.[7]

Guillaume points out that the Quran at first "had a large number of variants, not always trifling in significance."[8]

It is interesting to note that in scholarly Muslim journals, there is beginning to be a grudging acknowledgment of the fact that there are variant and conflicting readings on the text of the Quran.[9]

A Muslim Cover-Up

The work of Western scholars such as Arthur Jeffery and others has been hampered by Muslim reluctance to let Western scholars see old manuscripts of the Quran which are based on pre-Uthman texts. Jeffery relates one incident:

> An interesting modern example occurred during the last visit of the late Professor Berstrasser to Cairo. He was engaged in taking photographs for the Archive and had photographed a number of the early Kufic Codices in the Egyptian Library when I drew his attention to one in the Azhar Library that possessed certain curious features. He sought permission to photograph that also, but permission was refused and the Codex withdrawn from access, as it was not consistent with orthodoxy to allow a Western scholar to have knowledge of such a text.[10]

Jeffery comments:

> With regard to such variants as did survive there were definite efforts at suppression in the interests of orthodoxy.[11]

Some Verses Missing

According to Professor Guillaume in his book, *Islam*, (pp. 191ff.), some of the original verses of the Quran were lost.

For example, one Sura originally had 200 verses in the days of Ayesha. But by the time Uthman standardized the text of the Quran, it had only 73 verses! A total of 127 verses had been lost, and they have never been recovered.

The Shiite Muslims claim that Uthman left out 25 percent of the original verses in the Quran for political reasons.[12]

That there are verses which got left out of Uthman's version of the Quran is universally recognized.[13]

John Burton's book, *The Collection of the Quran*, which was published by Cambridge University, documents how such verses were lost.[14]

Burton states concerning the Muslim claim that the Quran is perfect:

> The Muslim accounts of the history of the Quran texts are a mass of confusion, contradiction and inconsistencies.[15]

Changes in the Quran

One interesting way that some of the original verses of the Quran were lost is that a follower of Muhammad named Abdollah Sarh would make suggestions to Muhammad about rephrasing, adding to, or subtracting from the Suras. Muhammad often did as Sarh suggested.

Ali Dashti explains what happened:

> Abdollah renounced Islam on the ground that the revelations, if from God, could not be changed at the prompting of a scribe such as he. After his apostasy he went to Mecca and joined the Qorayshites.[16]

It is no wonder that when Muhammad conquered Mecca one of the first people he killed was Abdollah, for he knew too much and opened his mouth too often.

Some Verses Abrogated

In the abrogation process spoken of earlier, verses which are contradictory to Muslim faith and practice have been removed from the text, such as the "satanic verses" in which Muhammad approved of the worship of the three goddesses, the daughters of Allah.

The Arabic scholar E. Wherry comments:

> There being some passages in the Quran which are contradictory, the Muhammadan doctors obviate any objection from thence by the doctrine of abrogation; for they say that God in the Quran commanded several things which were for good reasons afterwards revoked and abrogated.[17]

Wherry goes on to document numerous examples of verses taken out of the Quran.

Canon Sell in his work, *Historical Development of the Quran*, also comments on the practice of abrogating verses out of the Quran if they are troublesome:

> It is to us astounding how so compromising a procedure can have been permitted to be introduced into the system by friends and foes.[18]

Some Verses Added

Not only have parts of the Quran been lost, but entire verses and chapters have been added to it.

For example, Ubai had several Suras in his manuscript of the Quran which Uthman omitted from his standardized text.

Thus there were Qurans in circulation before Uthman's text which had additional revelations from Muhammad that Uthman did not find or approve of, and thus he failed to place them in his text.

No Originals

As to the claim that the original manuscript of the Quran is still in existence, we have already pointed out there was no single "manuscript" of the Quran.

As Arthur Jeffery has stated:

> Nothing is more certain than that when the Prophet died there was no collected, arranged, collated body of revelation. The earliest strata of tradition available to us make it quite certain that there was no Quran left ready as a heritage for the community. The Prophet had proclaimed his messages orally, and, except in the later period of his ministry, whether they were recorded or not was often a matter of chance.[19]

What about the Muslim claim that Muhammad had compiled a complete manuscript of the Quran before he died? Jeffery answers:

> Very little is needed to reveal the fact that this account is largely fictitious.[20]

Caesar Farah in his book on Islam, states:

> When Muhammed died there existed no singular codex of the sacred text.[21]

The *Shorter Encyclopedia of Islam* comments:

> One thing only is certain and is openly recognized by tradition, namely, that there was not in existence any collection of revelations in final form, because, as long as he was alive, new revelations were being added to the earlier ones.[22]

It is clear, therefore, that the bones, stones, palm leaves, tree bark, etc. which contained some of the material which Muhammad spoke after his seizures or trances were gathered together *after* his death.

It is also a fact that none of these things are in existence today. They have all long since been lost or perished.

The early versions of the Quran were in conflict with each other. Some had more or less Suras than others. The wording was often different.

On each occasion when we challenged a Muslim apologist to tell us the place where the "original" manuscript of the Quran was stored, he stated that he did not know where it was but that he was sure that it existed because it had to. Such an argument is worse than no argument at all!

Uthman's Text

As to the labor of the Caliph Uthman, the following historical questions must be asked:

1. Why did he have to standardize a common text if a standard text was already in existence?

2. Why did he try to destroy all the "other" manuscripts if there were no other conflicting manuscripts?

3. Why did he have to use the threat of death to force people to accept his text if everyone had the same text?

4. Why did many people reject his text in favor of their own texts?

These four questions reveal the utter state of confusion and contradiction that existed in the time of Uthman over the text of the Quran.

The fact that he ordered all of the older copies of the Quran destroyed reveals his fear that such copies would reveal that his own text was deficient either by addition to or subtraction from what Muhammad actually said.

Thankfully, some of these older materials have survived and have been recovered by such scholars as Arthur Jeffery.

Western scholars have shown beyond all reasonable doubt that Uthman's text did not contain all of the Quran. Neither was what it did contain correct in all of its wording.

Plenty of Translations

As to the Muslim claim that the Quran cannot be translated, it is amazing to us that the English Muslim Mohammed Pickthal could state, "The Koran cannot be translated" (p. vii), in the very introduction to his excellent translation of it!

The claim that the Quran cannot be translated is clearly refuted by the existence of many such translations.

Suras Like It Written

The challenge to produce Suras like those found in the Quran has been answered several times. The Middle East scholar Canon Sell comments:

> Men can produce its like in eloquence and arrangement. A man, named Nadir ibn Haritha, was bold enough to accept the challenge, and arranged some stories of the Persian kings in chapters and Suras and recited them.[23]

McClintock and Strong comment:

> Hamzah ben-Ahed wrote a book against the Koran with at least equal elegance, and Maslema another, which surpassed it, and

occasioned a defection of great number of Mussulmans.[24]

One last observation will be made in this chapter.

The Fingerprints of Muhammad

Since Muslims claim that the Quran was "handed down" from heaven, and that Muhammad cannot be viewed as its human author, it is interesting to point out that, according to the *Concise Encyclopedia of Islam*, the Arabic of the Quran is in the dialect and vocabulary of someone who was a member of the Quraysh tribe living in the city of Mecca. Thus Muhammad's fingerprints can be found all over the Quran.[25]

If the Quran were written in some kind of heavenly, perfect Arabic, why then does it clearly reveal that it was spoken by someone who was a member of the Quraysh tribe residing in Mecca?

We must submit that the argument of the Muslim at this point as to the Quran being written in heavenly Arabic falls to the ground.

The Quran, in its dialect, vocabulary, and content, reflects the style of its author, Muhammad—not some heavenly Allah.

Conclusion

The true history of the collection and the creation of the text of the Quran reveals that the Muslim claims are indeed fictitious and not in accord with the facts. The fingerprints of Muhammad can be seen on every page as a witness to its human origin.

A Scientific Examination of the Quran

It never ceases to amaze us that many modern Muslims feel that they have the perfect right and freedom to criticize the Bible as being corrupt and contradictory but whenever anyone dares to criticize the Quran along the same lines, they label this as rude, offensive, and racist!

Bucaille's Book

One example of this is Maurice Bucaille's book, *The Bible, the Quran and Science*. While Bucaille launches a full scale attack on the inspiration and text of the Bible, when it comes to the Quran, he assures the reader that it has "undisputed authenticity"!

He does not deal with the many problems found in the Quran but spends his time attacking the Bible.[1].

In reality, people have been disputing the Quran from the very beginning and are still disputing it today.

Several Problems

There are several problems with Bucaille's methodology.

First, both the Quran and the Hadith uphold the Bible as the inspired Word of God and frequently appeal to it as the authority for what Muhammad taught and did. Thus if the Bible is brought down, then the Quran and the Hadith will go down with it.[2]

Second, Bucaille violates one of the most basic laws of logic. Indeed, his book bristles with every logical error known to man. But in particular, he assumes that if he can "refute" the Bible, then the Quran is established.

You cannot, however, prove your own position by simply refuting someone else's position.

As a matter of logic, the Bible, the Quran, and the Hadith could all be wrong! The Quran is not inspired just because some other sacred book is refuted. Each book must stand or fall on its own merits.

Circular Reasoning

Some Muslims again use circular reasoning when it comes to the Quran. They assert as true what they have yet to prove.

Muslim: Muhammad is the prophet of God.

Non-Muslim: Why is this true?

Muslim: The Quran says so.

Non-Muslim: Why is the Quran true?

Muslim: Muhammad is the prophet of God.

Muslim: The Quran is without error.

Non-Muslim: Why is this true?

Muslim: Because the Quran says so.

Non-Muslim: But why is the Quran true?

Muslim: The Quran is without error.

Instead of endlessly rowing in a circle with only one oar, we must submit the Quran to a critical scientific examination. If it is true, it will stand up to any examination. But if it is false, it is better to know it now than to take a blind leap of faith.

The Gospel of Barnabas

The recent attempt of some Muslims to use the Gnostic work entitled the Gospel of Barnabas as if it were a long-lost gospel by the disciple that bears its name and more authoritative than the New Testament deserves a few comments.

Western scholars have repeatedly demonstrated that the so-called Gospel of Barnabas is a fraud in every respect.[3]

For example, Barnabas could not have written the book because its vocabulary reveals that it was not written in the first century.

More importantly, it contains statements that clearly contradict the teachings found in the Quran, the Hadith, and the Bible! It is a sword that cuts three ways!

Just as the Muslim can use this so-called lost gospel to contradict the Bible, non-Muslims can also use it to contradict the Quran and the Hadith.[4]

For example, the Gospel of Barnabas condemns having more than one wife while the Quran allows up to four wives. It also allows the eating of pork while the Quran condemns it.

For a Muslim to proclaim the inspiration of the Gospel of Barnabas is to figuratively put a knife to his own throat!

Freedom to Criticize

What Muslims must understand is that if they have the freedom to criticize the Bible, then other people have the same freedom to criticize the Quran. After all, "What is sauce for the gander is also sauce for the goose!"

Many Muslims feel that any criticism of the Quran is blasphemous and should not be allowed. This insight explains why Muslim apologists will not agree to debate the errors and the contradictions in the Quran. They want to debate Christianity, the Bible, etc. but never to defend the Quran itself.

Agreement Ahead of Time

After years of dealing with Muslims, we have found it essential at the outset to get their agreement to the fact that in the West we have religious freedom, which means that we have the right to criticize the Bible, the Quran, the Hadith, the Vedas, the Book of Mormon and any other "holy" book.

Not a Personal Slur

Such discussions should not be viewed as a personal attack or slur. They should be carried out in an objective and scholarly manner in order that the truth may be discovered.

Any religion which refuses to allow people to examine its sacred book using the normal rules of research and logic evidently has something to hide.

The Plain Truth

The plain truth is that the Quran contains many problems, some of which we will now point out.

Since the Quran claims to be free from all error as proof of its inspiration in Sura 85:21,22, the presence of just one error in the Quran is enough to cast serious doubt on that claim.

The Bible Versus the Quran

Throughout his early ministry, Muhammad constantly appealed to the Old and New Testament Scriptures as the basis and standard by which his teachings should be judged.

He would say that if you wanted to know whether he was speaking the truth, go to the people of the Book and ask them to look in their Scriptures to see whether or not what he was saying was true (Suras 2–13,16,17, 20, 21, 23, 25, 26, 28, 29, 32, 34, 35, 39–48, 53, 54, 61, 62, 66, 74,80,87,98, etc.).

The Principle Was Sound

The principle that Muhammad used in the beginning was a valid one. The older revelation must be the judge of all so-called new revelations.

Thus the Bible must be the standard which judges all new revelations including the Quran itself.

This is simply a point of chronology. Muhammad came 600 years after Jesus Christ. The Quran thus comes *after* the completion of the New Testament.

The Old Verified the New

The validity of the New Testament is based upon the fact of its fulfillment of the predictions, symbolism, and typology of the Old Testament.

In the same way, if the Quran is to be received as the Word of God, it must meet the test of being in complete compliance and accord with the Holy Scriptures as found in the Bible.

The Quran itself claims that it is a continuation of the Bible and it will not contradict it (Sura 2:136).

A Point of Logic

What this means in logic is that whenever the Bible and the Quran have a conflict or contradiction, the Quran is to give way, not the Bible.

This is particularly true when the text of the Quran contradicts the text of the Bible. The Muslim position is that the *same* God (Allah) revealed the Bible and the Quran.

Thus the Quran will never contradict the Bible, otherwise Allah would be contradicting himself.

It is only obvious that if Allah contradicted himself, he is not perfect. And if he is not perfect, then he cannot be God.

A Literary Comparison

This calls for a literary comparison of the text of the Bible and the text of the Quran.

It is not even necessary for someone to believe in the inspiration of the Bible to make a comparison between it and the Quran.

Logically speaking, an atheist, skeptic, Hindu, or Jew could make such a literary comparison just as well as a committed Christian.

Which Book Has Priority?

If the Quran does not correspond to the text and teachings of the Bible, then the Quran contradicts the Bible. If it contradicts the Bible, then the Quran must yield. Why?

Since the Bible was *before* the Quran and the Quran itself appeals to the Bible for verification, then whenever there is a conflict between the two, the newer and the lesser (the Quran) must give way to the older and the greater (the Bible).

Is the Bible Corrupt?

The Muslim answer to this approach is to say that the Quran is always right even when it disagrees with the Bible. Why? Because the Bible has been corrupted and cannot be trusted.

While it is easy to say that the text of the Bible is corrupt, it is another thing to prove it.

In countless encounters with Muslims, whenever the Quran contradicts some particular verse in the Bible, they have always said, "The Bible is corrupted at this point."

When I ask for some kind of proof that the Hebrew or Greek text is corrupt, they respond by saying, "I do not have to prove it is corrupt. It has to be corrupt, otherwise it would agree with the holy Quran."

For example, the Quran contradicts the Bible in that it denies that Jesus was crucified.

Now, is there any manuscript evidence that the verses in the Bible which speak of Christ's crucifixion were not originally in the Bible? Is there any textual evidence of any kind whatever that the Bible did not originally teach the crucifixion?

There is no evidence whatever that the biblical text was corrupted on the crucifixion. The Bible from the beginning clearly taught that Jesus died on the cross.[5]

A Logical Dilemma

The Muslim is trapped at this point. If he admits that the Bible originally said that Jesus died on the cross, then the Quran is in direct conflict with the older revelations.

But Muhammad promised that this would not happen. Why? The Quran must agree with the older revelations because they all supposedly came from the same God.

On the one hand, if the Muslim rejects the Bible, he must also reject the Quran because it appeals to the Bible as God's Word.

On the other hand, if he accepts the Bible, he still must reject the Quran because it contradicts the Bible. Either way, the Quran loses.

A Blind Leap of Faith

So what does the Muslim do? He takes a blind leap of faith and says, "The text of the Bible at this place must be corrupted. It did not originally teach that Jesus was crucified. I do not have to prove it. I know it is so because otherwise I am trapped and I will have to give up the Quran because it appeals to the Bible as the basis of its own authority."

The unreasonableness of the Muslim's argument grates against the scientific mind.

If there is not a shred of evidence that a particular text in the Bible has suffered any manuscript corruption, then it is irrational to say that it is corrupt just because it disagrees with the Quran.

Muslims answer this problem by saying that the Bible was corrupted *after* the Quran was written.

But since we have manuscripts of the Old Testament from as early as 200 B.C. and portions of the New Testament from the first century, we *know* what the Bible was like during the life of Jesus and the apostles.

When we compare this uncorrupted Bible with the mixed-up accounts, names, and speeches found in the Quran, the Quran is shown to be false.

It must also be pointed out that the Muslims argue that the Quran must be perfect because God would preserve His Word infallibly.

Yet if God failed to do this for the Bible, as they claim, why should He do this for the Quran?

The Higher Authority

Logically speaking, the Bible must be preferred above the Quran not only because it was *before* the Quran but also because the Quran appeals to the Bible as the already established higher authority.

A Scientific Examination

With these few introductory words, we will now proceed to a scientific examination of the Quran.

Since the Quran has so many problems, we will limit ourselves to approximately 100 of the most obvious ones.

How Many Days of Creation?

The very first problem in the Quran concerns the number of days it took God to create the world.

When you add up all the days mentioned in Sura 41:9,10,12 the Quran says that it took God *eight* days to create the world (4 days + 2 days + 2 days = 8 days).

But it only took *six* days according to the Bible (Genesis 1:31). Thus the Quran begins its contradiction of the Bible in the very first chapter of the Bible.

A Muslim friend objected to this, stating that the Hebrew text of the Bible was no doubt corrupted at this point and that it originally said that the creation took eight days.

I pointed out that there was no evidence in the Hebrew manuscripts of any corruption. Also, the Bible elsewhere says that the world was created in six days (Exodus 20:11).

Then I pointed out that the Quran in Suras 7:51 and 10:3 agreed with the biblical account that the creation of the world took only six days.

If six days is wrong, then the Quran in Suras 7 and 10 is wrong. But if eight days is wrong, then Sura 41 is wrong.

Using classic Muslim reasoning, he responded that then the Quran did not say eight days.

I added up the days mentioned in Sura 41 as $4 + 2 + 2 = 8$.

He then added it up and came up with $4 + 2 + 2 = 6$ "because 4 is divisible by 2 and hence 4 is actually a 2"!

When I pointed out that the Arabic said 4 and not 2, it did not faze him. He argued that $4 = 2$, otherwise he would be trapped into having to admit that the Quran was in error.

Thus he made the utterly ridiculous statement that $4 = 2$ rather than simply accepting the fact that Muhammad made an error at this point.

Noah, the Flood, and His Sons

According to the Bible, all three sons of Noah went into the ark with him and were saved from the flood (Genesis 7:1,7,13).

Yet, the Quran in Sura 11:32-48 says that one of the sons refused to go into the ark and was drowned in the flood!

Sura 11:44 also claims that the Ark came to rest on top of Mount Judi while the Bible says Mount Ararat. These contradictions cannot be clearer.

Mistakes About Abraham

The Quran makes many errors concerning Abraham:

1. The Quran says that Abraham's father's name was Azar, but the Bible says his name was Terah (Sura 6:74).

2. He did not live and worship in the valley of Mecca (Sura 14:37) but in Hebron according to the Bible.

3. It was his son Isaac that he went to sacrifice and not Ishmael as the Quran says (Sura 37:100-112).

4. He had eight sons and not just two as the Quran claims.

5. He had three wives and not two as the Quran says.

6. He did not build the Kabah, even though the Quran says so in Sura 2:125-127.

7. He was not thrown into a fire by Nimrod as the Quran claims in Suras 21:68,69 and 9:69.

This last error is most serious because it reveals a very frequent problem in the Quran.

Nimrod lived many centuries before Abraham. How then did Nimrod manage to throw Abraham into a fire when Nimrod had been dead for centuries?

Linear Time

The seventh-century Arab, and Muhammad in particular, did not think in terms of linear time, that is, historical chronology.

In the West, people think of history in terms of a straight line with a beginning, a middle, and an end.

In the East, people think of time in terms of never-ending cycles.

Evidently, in the Middle East at the time of Muhammad, Arabs did not have any settled conception of time at all.

Arab stories and legends put together places, people, and events in one present vision as if they were all living at the same time!

This is why throughout the Quran, Nimrod and Abraham, Haman and Moses, Mary and Aaron, etc. were all pictured as living and working together.

This is why the Quran can put together the flood and Moses, the tower of Babel and Pharoah, etc. as if all those things happened at the same time.

This is a very serious challenge to the integrity of the Quran because it violates the historical chronology of the Bible and secular history at the same time.

Mistakes About Joseph

The Quran makes the mistake of saying that the man who bought Joseph, Jacob's son, was named Aziz (Sura 12:21ff.) when his name was really Potiphar (Genesis 37:36).

Biblical Characters

The Quran makes the same kind of error when it refers to Goliath as Jalut, Korah as Karun, Saul as Talut, Enoch as Idris, Ezekiel as Dhu'l-Khifl, John the Baptist as Yahya, Jonah as Yunus, etc.

Since Muhammad did not have access to the Bible (an Arabic translation of the Bible was not in existence at that time) he frequently got the names, events, and chronology all wrong.

As pagan, Jewish, and Christian traders sat around the fire telling each other their favorite stories, they would get the names, times, and events all jumbled up and confused.

Encyclopedia Britannica states:

> The deviations from the biblical narratives are very marked, and can in most cases be traced back to the legendary anecdotes of the Jewish Haggada and the Apocryphal Gospels. Much has been written concerning the sources from which Mohammed derived this information; there is no evidence that he was able to read, and his dependence on oral communication may explain some of his misconceptions; e.g., the confusion of Haman, the minister of Ahasuerus, with the minister of Pharoah (xl,38), and the identification of Miriam, the sister of Moses, with Mary (Miryam), the mother of Jesus.[6]

Muhammad's gross misunderstandings of biblical stories and doctrines reflect only a hearsay knowledge. As the great Arabic scholar Canon Edward Sell pointed out concerning these erroneous names:

> He certainly did not get them from the Old Testament. The confusion of names is quite remarkable.[7]

Mistakes About Moses

The Quran contains many errors concerning Moses:

1. It was not Pharoah's *wife* who adopted Moses as the Quran claims in Sura 28:8,9. It was actually Pharoah's *daughter* (Exodus 2:5).

2. Noah's flood did not take place in Moses' day (Sura 7:136, compare 7:59ff.). This error cannot be easily swept aside.

3. The Quran says that Haman lived in Egypt during the time of Moses and worked for Pharoah building the tower of Babel (Suras 27:4-6; 28:38; 29:39; 40:23,24,36,37). But Haman actually lived in Persia and was in the service of King Ahasuerus. See the book of Esther for details.[8] This is a very serious error as it not only contradicts the Bible but secular history as well.

4. Crucifixion was not used in the time of Pharoah although the Quran says so in Sura 7:124.

Mistakes About Mary

The Quran contains many errors concerning Mary, the mother of Jesus:

1. Her father's name was not Imram (Sura 66:12).

2. She did not give birth to Jesus under a palm tree but in a stable (Sura 19:22 versus Luke 2:1-20).

3. Muhammad confused the mother of Jesus with the Mary who was the sister of Moses and Aaron (Sura 19:28).[9] This is a very serious error as it reveals that Muhammad had no understanding of the different time periods for biblical figures.

4. Muhammad clearly made up fraudulent speeches and miracles for her in Sura 19:23-26.

5. Zacharias could not speak the entire time until his son was born, not just for three days as the Quran claims (Sura 19:10 versus Luke 1:20).

Fictional Speeches

Muhammad made up fictional speeches of people in the Bible using such words as "Muslim" and "Islam" which were not in the languages of the people supposedly quoted at that time.

This would be as ridiculous as claiming that Muhammad said, "I like Kentucky Fried Chicken best."

Obviously, such terminology did not exist in Muhammad's time! And neither did the terminology Muhammad put into the mouths of biblical figures.

All of the speeches attributed to Abraham, Isaac, Jacob, Noah, Moses, Mary, Jesus, etc. contain words and phrases which clearly reveal that they are frauds (Suras 2:60,126-128,132-133,260; 3:49-52,67; 6:74-82; 7:59-63, 120-126; 10:71,72; 18:60-70; 19:16-33; etc.).

The Water Test

The test of how the soldiers drank water from a stream did not take place in the days of Saul when David defeated Goliath but many years earlier with Gideon. Compare Sura 2:249,250 with Judges 7:1-8.

Secular History Mistakes

The Quran contains clear historical mistakes:

1. One example would be in Sura 105 where Muhammad claims that the elephant army of Abrah was defeated by birds dropping stones of baked clay upon them.

   According to the historical record, Abrah's army withdrew their attack on Mecca after smallpox broke out among the troops.[10]

2. The Kabah was not built by Adam and then rebuilt by Abraham. It was built by pagans to worship a black rock which fell out of the sky. Abraham never lived at Mecca.

3. In Sura 20:87,95 we are told that the Jews made the golden calf in the wilderness at the suggestion of "the Samaritan."

This is a clear historical error as such a country and a people by that name did not exist during the time frame of the passage.

Samaria did not come into existence for many centuries, until *after* the captivity of Israel first by the Assyrians and then by the Babylonians.

Yusuf Ali tries to get away from this error by obscuring the translation of the name, but the Arabic is clear.

4. One of the greatest errors in the Quran concerns Alexander the Great, who is called Zul-qarnain.

   The Quran claims that he was a Muslim who worshiped Allah and that he lived to an old age (Sura 18:89-98).

   This error is ironclad as the historical evidence concerning Alexander makes it clear that Alexander was not a Muslim and he did not live to an old age.

   Encyclopedia Britannica states:

   > His [Muhammad's] account of Alexander, introduced as "the two horned one" (xviii,82), is derived from the Romance of Alexander, which was current among the Nestorian Christians of the 7th Century in a Syriac version.[11]

In the light of this obvious historical error, some modern Muslims have argued that the Quran is not speaking of Alexander.

But based on the historic orthodox Muslim interpretation of this passage, even Yusuf Ali has to admit:

> I have not the least doubt that Zul-qarnain is meant to be Alexander the Great, the historic Alexander, and not some legendary Alexander.[12]

The *Concise Dictionary of Islam* also upholds the view that Alexander the Great is the subject in this passage.[13]

Scientific Problems

The Quran contains scientific errors. For example, it claims that Alexander the Great followed the setting of the sun and found that it went down into the waters of a muddy spring (Sura 18:85,86).

Self-Contradictions

The Quran contradicts *itself* in many ways. Since the Quran claims in Sura 39:23,28 to be free from all contradictions, just one contradiction is sufficient to show that it is not God's Word.

1. As we have already shown, the Quran gives us four conflicting accounts of Muhammad's reception of the Quran:

   • We are first told that Allah came to Muhammad in the form of a man and that Muhammad saw him (Suras 53:2-18; 81:19-24).

   • Then we are told that it was "the holy Spirit" who came to Muhammad (Suras 16:102; 26:192-194).

   • Later on, the Quran says that the angels were the ones who came down to Muhammad (Sura 15:8).

   • The last and most popular version is that it was the angel Gabriel who delivered the Quran to Muhammad (Sura 2:97).

2. The Quran differs on whether a day is a thousand years or fifty thousand years in God's sight (Sura 32:5 versus 70:4).

3. In Suras 2:58 and 7:161 the same quotation is given with conflicting wording. This is one of many such examples of this problem.

   The presence of conflicting wording is serious because the Muslims claim that the Quran is absolutely perfect even in its quotations.

   Christians do not make such claims for the Bible but view the speeches found in the Bible as summaries of what was said. Thus different Gospel writers summarized the sermons of Jesus in different words, which is perfectly normal.

4. At first Muhammad told his followers to face Jerusalem in prayer. Then he told them since God was everywhere they could face any way they wanted. Then he changed his mind yet again and directed them to pray toward Mecca (Sura 2:115 versus 2:144).

   Many scholars believe that the changes in direction were dependent on whether he was trying to please the Jews or the pagans.[14]

5. Muhammad first started out saying that his followers could defend themselves if attacked (Sura 22:39). Then he commanded them to go to war on his behalf (Sura 2:216-218). This was to gain wealth by robbing caravans. But as his army grew, so did his thirst for plunder (Sura 5:33). So he ordered wars to persecute other religions as well as to gain more wealth (Sura 9:5,29).

   Allah's will seems to change according to Muhammad's success in killing and looting.[15]

6. Who was the first to believe? Abraham or Moses (Sura 6:14 versus 7:143)? You can't have two "firsts."

7. The fact that Judaism and Christianity broke up into different sects was used in the Quran to

prove that they were not of God (Suras 30:30-32; 42:13,14).

Yet Islam has itself broken up into many warring sects and therefore cannot be true if the Quran is right.

Convenient Revelations

The Quran contains convenient revelations for the personal gain or pleasure of Muhammad:

- When Muhammad wanted his adopted son's wife, he suddenly got a revelation from Allah declaring it permissible to take another man's wife (Sura 33:36-38).

- When he wanted more wives or wanted to stop his wives from quarreling, he got a quick revelation for it (Sura 33:28-34).

- When people bothered him at his house, he received convenient revelations setting up rules concerning when to visit him and when not to bother him (Suras 33:53-58; 29:62-63; 49:1-5).

Legendary Materials

Muhammad used much legendary and fanciful material as sources for the Quran.[16]

As Professor Jomier, one of France's greatest Middle East scholars, points out:

> Moslems receive these narratives as the word of God, without inquiring about their historical background. In fact we have there a popular, poetic form of legends, variants of religious themes known from other sources.[17]

Arabian Sources

The Quran repeats fanciful Arabian fables as if they were true.

- Arabic legends about the fabulous jinns fill its pages.[18]

- The story of the she-camel who leapt out of a rock and became a prophet was known long before Muhammad (Suras 7:73-77,85; 91:14; 54:29).

- The story of an entire village of people who were turned into apes because they broke the sabbath by fishing was a popular legend in Muhammad's day (Suras 2:65; 7:163-166).

- The gushing 12 springs story found in Sura 2:60 comes from pre-Islamic legends.

- In what is called the "Rip Van Winkle" story, seven men and their animals slept for 309 years in a cave and then woke up perfectly fine (Sura 18:9-26)!

  This legend is found in Greek and Christian fables as well as Arabian lore.

- The fable of the pieces of four dead, cut-up birds getting up and flying was well known in Muhammad's time (Sura 2:260).

It is also clear that Muhammad used such pre-Islamic literature as the Saba Moallaqat of Imra'ul Cays in his composition of Suras 21:96; 29:31,46; 37:59; 54:1, and 93:1.

Jewish Sources

Many of the stories in the Quran come from the Jewish Talmud, the Midrash, and many apocryphal works.

This was pointed out by Abraham Geiger in 1833, and further documented by another Jewish scholar, Dr. Abraham Katsh, of New York University, in 1954.[19]

1. The source of Sura 3:35-37 is the fanciful book called *The Protevangelion's James the Lesser*.

2. The source of Sura 87:19 is the Testament of Abraham.

3. The source of Sura 27:17-44 is the Second Targum of Esther.

4. The fantastic tale that God made a man "die for a hundred years" with no ill effects on his food, drink, or donkey was a Jewish fable (Sura 2:259ff.).

5. The idea that Moses was resurrected and other material came from the Jewish Talmud (Sura 2:55,56,67).

6. The story in Sura 5:30,31 can also be found in pre-Islamic works from Pirke Rabbi Eleazer, the Targum of Jonathan ben Uzziah and the Targum of Jerusalem.

7. The tale of Abraham being delivered from Nimrod's fire came from the Midrash Rabbah (see Suras 21:51-71; 29:16,17; 37:97,98).

   It must be also pointed out that Nimrod and Abraham did not live at the same time. Muhammad was always mixing people together in the Quran who did not live at the same time.

8. The non-biblical details of the visit of the Queen of Sheba (Saba) in Sura 27:20-44 came from the Second Targum of the Book of Esther.

9. The source of Sura 2:102 is no doubt the Midrash Yalkut (chapter 44).

10. The story found in Sura 7:171 of God lifting up Mount Sinai and holding it over the heads of the Jews as a threat to squash them if they rejected the law came from the Jewish book Abodah Sarah.

11. The story of the making of the golden calf in the wilderness, in which the image jumped out of the fire fully formed and actually mooed (Suras 7:148; 20:88), came from Pirke Rabbi Eleazer.

12. The seven heavens and hells described in the Quran came from the Zohar and the Hagigah.

13. Muhammad utilized the Testament of Abraham to teach that a scale or balance will be used on the day of judgment to weigh good and bad deeds in order to determine whether one goes to heaven or hell (Suras 42:17; 101:6-9).

Heretical Christian Sources

One of the most documented and damaging facts about the Quran is that Muhammad used heretical "Christian" Gnostic gospels and their fables for material in the Quran.

Encyclopedia Britannica comments:

> The gospel was known to him chiefly through apocryphal and heretical sources.[20]

This has been demonstrated many times by various scholars.[21]

For example, in Suras 3:49 and 100:110, the baby Jesus speaks from the cradle! Later on, the Quran has Jesus making clay birds come alive.

The Bible tells us that the *first* miracle Jesus did was at the wedding at Cana (John 2:11).

Sabean Sources

Muhammad incorporated parts of the religion of the Sabeans into Islam.[22]

He adopted such pagan rituals as:

- Worshiping at the Kabah
- Praying five times a day toward Mecca (Muhammad chose five of the same times the Sabeans prayed.)
- Fasting for part of a day for an entire month

Eastern Religious Sources

Muhammad derived some of his ideas from Eastern religions such as Zoroastrianism and Hinduism. All of these things were in existence long before Muhammad was born.

The Quran records the following things which are ascribed to Muhammad but in reality were previously known stories now attributed to him for the first time:[23]

- The story of a flying trip through seven heavens
- The Houries of paradise
- Azazil and other spirits coming up from hades
- The "light" of Muhammad
- The bridge of Sirat
- Paradise with its wine, women, and song (from the Persians)
- The king of death
- The peacock story

Mistakes About Jesus

The Quran contradicts the Bible's teaching on the

person and work of Jesus Christ by saying in Suras
4:157; 5:19,75; 9:30:

- Jesus was not the Son of God.
- He did not die for our sins.
- He was not crucified.
- He was not divine as well as human.
- He is not the Savior.[24]

The utter contradiction between the biblical and
quranic view of Jesus cannot be easily dismissed. This is
clearly not an issue of corruption but of contradiction. It
is one of the fundamental issues which will forever
divide Christianity from Islam.

Mistakes About the Trinity

The Quran contains many errors about what Christians believe and practice.

One of the most significant is that the Quran mis-
represents the Christian doctrine of the Trinity.

Muhammad mistakenly thought that Christians
worshiped three gods: the Father, the Mother (Mary),
and the Son (Jesus), (Sura 5:73-75,116).[25]

As Richard Bell pointed out:

> [Muhammad] never understood the doc-
> trine of the Trinity.[26]

Encyclopedia Britannica states:

> [There are] mistaken concepts of the Trin-
> ity in the Quran.[27]

Yusuf Ali's translation of the Quran tries to avoid
this error by deliberately mistranslating Sura 5:73.

The Arabic text condemns those who say that
"Allah is the third of three," that is to say Allah is only

one of three gods! Both Arberry and Pickthall translate this correctly.

Ali mistranslates Sura 5:73 to read:

> They do blaspheme who say: God is one of three in a Trinity.

The words "in a Trinity" are not in the Arabic text. Ali puts it in his translation in an attempt to avoid the rather obvious error that Christians believe in three gods.

In reality, Christians believe only in one God who is in three persons: the Father, the Son, and the Holy Spirit. They do not believe that Mary is a part of the Trinity.

Even the *Concise Dictionary of Islam* admits:

> In some cases the "material" which forms the substance of Quranic narrative, details of the creeds of Christianity and Judaism for example, does not correspond to those religion's own understanding of their beliefs. This could be said, for example, of the notion of the Trinity found in the Quran, the story of Satan's refusal to bow down to Adam, the Docetist view of the crucifixion, all of which can be traced to the dogmas of Gnostic sects, which are heretical in relationship to orthodox Christianity and Judaism. The Trinity "seen" in the Quran is not the Trinity of the Apostles Creed, or of the Nicene Creed.[28]

The Quran is so clearly erroneous at this point that Muslims such as Yusuf Ali must mistranslate the Quran to get away from it!

Mistakes About the "Son" of God

The Quran also makes the mistake of saying that Christians believe Jesus is the "Son" of God in the sense that God the "Father" has a male body and had sexual intercourse with Mary.

In Muhammad's mind, to say that God had a son was to blaspheme because it meant that God had sex with a woman (Suras 2:116; 6:100,101; 10:68; 16:57; 19:35; 23:91; 37:149, 157; 43:16-19).

Christians believe that Mary was a virgin when Jesus was conceived in her by the Holy Spirit (Luke 1:35).

Thus Jesus is the "Son" of God, but not in the sexual sense that Muhammad understood. God the "Father" is not a man and hence does not have a male body and has not had sex with anyone. The Quran is 100 percent wrong on this issue.

Praying Toward Jerusalem

The Quran makes the mistake of teaching that Christians bow in prayer toward Jerusalem (Sura 2:144, 145). Christians do not bow toward any place on earth when in prayer.

Is Allah the Name of Christ?

Christians do not claim that Allah is the name of the Messiah or the Christ as Sura 5:72 claims. They believe in one God in three persons and that Jesus Christ was human as well as divine.

Mistakes About Jewish Beliefs

The Quran makes the mistake of claiming that the Jews believed that Ezra was the Son of God, the Messiah, just as Christians claim that Jesus was (Sura 9:30). Nothing could be further from the truth.

As the *Concise Dictionary of Islam* points out:

> There are many details regarding Judaism
> which are in variance with Jewish belief.[29]

Arab Racism

According to the literal Arabic translation of Sura
3:106,107, on Judgment Day, only people with white
faces will be saved. People with black faces will be
damned. This is racism in its worse form!

As Victor and Deborah Khalil point out in their
article on Islam:

> American blacks have been widely wooed
> by Islam, but through misinformation. They
> hear, "Christianity is the white man's re-
> ligion; Islam is the religion of all mankind."
> They are told that Allah and Mohammed
> are black. In reality, Muslims in the Middle
> East still regard blacks as slaves. It would
> be worse than blasphemy for them to be-
> lieve that either Allah or Mohammed were
> black.[30]

It must be also pointed out that Arab Muslims were
enslaving black Africans long before Westerners, to
their shame, got involved.

A Carnal Heaven

The Quran promises a heaven full of wine and free
sex (Suras 2:25; 4:57; 11:23; 47:15).

If drunkeness and gross immorality is sinful on
earth, how is it right in Paradise?

Is this not yet more proof that Islam reflects the
ideas and customs of seventh-century Arab culture?

The Quran's picture of paradise is exactly what a seventh-century pagan Arab would have thought wonderful.

The carnal concept of a harem of beautiful women and all the wine you can drink is in direct conflict with the spirituality and holiness of the biblical concept of heaven (Revelation 22:12-17). The contradiction cannot be clearer.

The Problem of Usury

In seventh-century Arabia, the practice of charging interest on money that was loaned to people was condemned as usury. Thus, it is no surprise to learn that Muhammad likewise condemned usury in the Quran (Suras 2:275ff.; 3:130; 4:161; 30:39).

The reason we point this out is that modern Muslims openly disobey the Quran at this point. Muslims will now charge interest on the money they loan out, and they will pay interest on the money they borrow.

If the Muslims were to apply the Quran's condemnation of usury to their modern-day financial practices, there would be no Muslim banks. Not even Muslim governments would charge interest or receive interest on any loans.

This is why some Muslim apologists try desperately to stay clear of the issue of usury, or else they try to define usury as taking unjust interest.

But it is clear, not only from the Quran, but also from the historical context, that Muhammad was prohibiting the charging of *any* interest at all on money that was loaned out, particularly to fellow Muslims.

An Interesting Discussion

In one conversation with a Muslim, I brought up the Quran's condemnation of charging interest on the money lent out to others. He dismissed this because he claimed that the Quran at that point was only reflecting seventh-century Arabian culture and therefore could be disregarded!

Then I pointed out that if this same principle was applied to all the other cultural elements within Islam, such as the five pillars, civil laws, dietary laws, dress codes, etc. Islam itself would collapse like a house of cards. After digesting this, he stated that the Quran's condemnation of usury was not a "cultural" law but the eternal law of Allah.

I could not help but point out that the Quran's condemnation of usury was either cultural and hence could be disobeyed or it was the eternal word of Allah and he would have to give up any interest-bearing accounts he had.

To this he gave no response.

To the rational mind, it is clear that every time a Muslim accepts interest payments on his bank accounts, loans, or mortgages he is demonstrating to one and all that the Quran is really the product of seventh-century Arabian culture and not the eternal Word of God.

Conclusion

While the devout Muslim believes with all of his heart that the rituals and doctrines of Islam are entirely heavenly in origin and thus cannot have any earthly sources, Middle East scholars have demonstrated beyond all doubt that every ritual and belief in Islam can be traced back to pre-Islamic Arabian culture.

In other words, Muhammad did not preach anything new. Everything he taught had been believed and practiced in Arabia long before he was ever born. Even the idea of "only one God" was borrowed from the Jews and the Christians.

This irrefutable fact casts to the ground the Muslim claim that Islam was revealed from heaven. Since its rituals, beliefs, and even the Quran itself can be fully explained in terms of pre-Islamic sources in Arabian culture, this means that the religion of Islam is false.

It is no surprise, therefore, that Western scholars have concluded that Allah is not God, Muhammad was not his prophet, and the Quran is not the Word of God.

PART SIX

THE NATION
OF ISLAM

Eleven

The Black Muslim Movement in America*

We cannot conclude our discussion of Islam without dealing with the history and teachings of the Nation of Islam, whose followers are known as black Muslims.

At the outset, we acknowledge that orthodox Islam does not want to be identified with the black Muslim movement in America, which it condemns as spurious and heretical. Black Muslims are not viewed by orthodox Muslims as true Muslims or as part of Islam.

But given the inroads the black Muslims have made in the black community in America and the fact that they are now sending missionaries to Africa to convert other blacks to their message, it would be unwise to ignore them.

---

* I wish to acknowledge the valuable and insightful contributions of Professor Colin Akridge who is a black scholar in the field of comparative religions with a special emphasis on American cults and sects. It was our pleasure to work with him in the research and writing of this chapter.

Elijah Muhammad

Since Elijah Muhammad was the most well-known leader of what is now called the Nation of Islam, it is important to understand the background and beliefs of this man who so profoundly influenced the black community in the United States.

Early Life

Elijah Muhammad was not always known by that name. He was born on October 10, 1897 under the name of Elijah Poole, the son of Wali and Marie Poole.

Elijah's father was a Baptist pastor who sought to raise his children in the Christian faith. But one of his 13 children would eventually do everything in his power to destroy the gospel that his father and mother had always loved and preached. This erring child was none other than Elijah Poole.

A Fateful Meeting

After moving from his native state of Georgia to Detroit, Michigan in 1931, Elijah Poole came under the influence of a colorful religious teacher by the name of Wallace D. Fard.

Wallace D. Fard

Not much is known about Fard except that he was a peddler of "African" clothing who claimed to be "a brother from the East."

Some black Muslims claim that he was born in Mecca but they have never produced any documentation to prove this.

Seeking to give his followers an African identity and pride, he urged them to renounce their birth names and to adopt Muslim names such as Muhammad.

He also told them to dress like the Arab Muslims did in the Middle East. Of course, he was the one to sell them the robes and other items they needed.

Under Fard's influence, Elijah renounced the Christian faith of his parents and his birth name. Fard then gave him the Arab name of Karriem.

The Watchtower and Islam

The source of much of what Fard had to say about the Christian Church and its doctrines came from the teachings of the Watchtower Bible and Tract Society, or, as they are commonly known, the Jehovah's Witnesses.

The Watchtower denied all the essential teachings of historic Christianity such as the Trinity and went from house to house proclaiming that Jesus Christ was only a human prophet and *not* divine in any sense.

The Watchtower's denial of the Trinity and its reduction of Jesus to mere humanity laid the foundation for Fard to introduce his unique brand of Islam.

Going from house to house using Watchtower literature, Fard tore down his black followers' faith in the gospel of Jesus Christ.

The White Man's Religion

Having accomplished the first part of his task, he introduced Islam as the next logical step to get away from Christianity, which he mocked as "the white man's religion."

Of course, since Fard was himself a white man, this would lead one to conclude that the Nation of Islam was just another "white man's religion" also. It is interesting that black Muslims today are following the religion of a white man whom, like in the days of slavery, they call *Master* Fard Muhammad!

Fard's Plan

Fard's plan was simple. He took them from the Watchtower to Islam, from the Bible to the Quran and from Jesus to Muhammad. And the driving force which fueled this process was racism.

Black Racism

Fard taught that the white race was the "devil" while the black race was divine. He went so far as to say that black people were gods because they were black!

This, of course, would mean that Fard himself was a "white" devil. But this obvious problem is never answered by black Muslims.

Despite the obvious absurdity of Fard's teaching, it was appealing to those blacks who keenly felt oppressed and needed a way to rebel against what they identified as "the man." Accepting Fard's religion was one way to strike back at the white man.

Given the horrors and injustices that black people have suffered under white racism, Fard used black racism as the bait on the hook to draw them into his religion. Of course, he did not bother to tell them that Islam has always been as racist as any white society.

Elijah Takes Over

Wallace D. Fard suddenly disappeared in 1934. What happened to him remains a mystery. Many think that he was murdered to get him out of the way.

Regardless of why or how he disappeared, his demise gave Elijah the perfect opportunity to take over the black Muslim movement. It was at this time that his name was changed to Muhammad from Karriem.

Under Elijah Muhammad's guidance, the movement grew and became wealthy beyond his wildest dreams. This was due to the natural genius and organizational skills of Elijah Muhammad, who went so far as to repay his master by proclaiming that Fard was Allah incarnate!

Basic Teachings

The basic beliefs of black Muslims are found in Elijah Muhammad's two books, *The Supreme Wisdom*, and *The Message to the Black Man in America*.

Farrakhan's New Teachings

But it must be also pointed out in all fairness that today Louis Farrakhan has gone way beyond the teachings of both Fard and Elijah Muhammad and is now teaching his own unique doctrines.

Thus the reader must keep in mind that the present beliefs of black Muslims are a combination of the teachings of Wallace Fard, Elijah Muhammad, and Louis Farrakhan.

Farrakhan Takes a Ride

For example, during his 1991 Savior's Day sermon, Louis Farrakhan spoke of his encounter with a giant plane shaped like the wheel described in the book of Ezekiel. Its "eyes" were actually thousands of people looking out the windows.

This wheel-shaped plane is in orbit forty miles above the earth and is what some people would call a UFO.

Farrakhan stated that he was taken on board and went for a ride in this heavenly vessel.

While he was aboard, he heard the voice of none other than Master Elijah Muhammad—which supposedly proves that he is not dead but alive—and it was Elijah who built this mighty ship!

This "wheel" ship would one day destroy the white man and usher in the day of black power.

Farrakhan also claimed that 1,500 little planes from this giant "wheel" follow him at all times!

Neither Wallace Fard nor Elijah Muhammad ever taught such things!

The Nature of God

There is much confusion and contradiction in the black Muslim concept of God.

On the one hand, they state that there is only one God, whose proper name is Allah.

This sounds on the surface to be the basic creed of Islam. But the "Allah" in which the black Muslims believe is radically different from the Allah of Islam as well as the God of Judaism and Christianity.

The Allah of Islam is an eternal, uncreated, immaterial being. Allah is not begotten nor does he begat. Thus he is *not* a man.

Likewise, the Bible teaches in Numbers 23:19, "God is not a man."

But the black Muslim concept of God *as a man* is neither Jewish, Christian, nor Islamic!

According to Louis Farrakhan, "Allah" created himself out of a darkness that is material in nature. This material is "electricity."

Farrakhan teaches that Allah is not uncreated, immaterial, or invisible in the sense of being a spirit. God is a man of flesh and blood. He is a real human being.

Many Gods

Although he stated at the beginning of his sermon during the 1991 Savior's Day celebration that he bore witness that there was only one God, later on in the same sermon, Farrakhan stated that the "24 elders" mentioned in the book of Revelation were great scientists who were actually gods!

He went on to say that 12 of these elders were "major" scientists and gods. Among them was one supreme being or god who is over this particular time period. Farrakhan even used the phrase "a temporary god."

One of these major scientist gods created the moon by blowing up the earth. Later on he made the white man out of his evil side.

It would seem that Farrakhan's professed monotheism means only that there is one temporary god for this world *at this time*. But is this monotheism?

This is actually polytheism and more in line with the theology of Mormonism than with Judaism, Christianity, or Islam.

God Is a Man

According to black Muslim theology, Allah is a man—and none other than Master Wallace D. Fard Muhammad. He was Allah in human form!

This part of their creed is found in point 12 of the statement of faith which is usually printed on the back of their newspaper, *The Final Call*:

> 12. We believe that Allah (God) appeared in the Person of Master W. Fard Muhammad, July, 1930; the long-awaited "Messiah" of the Christians and the "Mahdi" of the Muslims.

Once again, while Mormonism has always taught that God was a man of flesh and blood, Judaism, Christianity, and Islam have always believed in the immaterial and nonhuman nature of God.

Different Manifestations

When Fard died, Allah did not die with him. God then manifested himself in Elijah Muhammad who was revealed to be the long-awaited "Messiah" of the Jews, the "Jesus" of the Christians, and the "Mahdi" of the Muslims!

Different Forms

While the physical form (the man) in which Allah manifests himself may die, Allah himself cannot die. He simply manifests himself in a new human form through whom he reveals his wisdom and truth.

While both Bahaism and Hinduism teach that God reveals himself in a series of incarnations, this is absolutely denied by Judaism, Christianity, and Islam.

The 1991 Savior's Day

Who is the present manifestation of Allah? In the 1991 "Savior's Day" celebration, Louis Farrakhan was introduced as the fulfillment of Isaiah 9:6-8. He was proclaimed as the "child who would be born" and the "son who would be given" because he was "Wonderful, Counselor, the Mighty God, the Prince of peace," etc.!

It was stated that Farrakhan healed the sick and made the blind see. It was implied clearly that Farrakhan was now "God manifested in the flesh."

The Christian "Spook"

The Christian doctrine of the invisible and spiritual nature of God was denounced as a lie. God was a man and not some kind of "spook."

On the Bible

Elijah Muhammad did not have much respect for the Bible. He warned his followers that the Bible was pure "poison" because it had been corrupted by the white man. The Quran was far superior.

He went so far as to call the Bible a "graveyard of the black man" because it was used by white people to keep black people down.

Farrakhan, however, holds up the Bible as the Word of God and quotes from it far more times than he quotes from the Quran.

His sermons at times are so filled with biblical texts and imagery that one would think he was in a Christian church!

On Jesus

Elijah Muhammad's Jesus was not a white man but a black African. He was only a mortal man like the Arab prophet Muhammad. People should no longer look to a "dead" Jesus according to Elijah.

Farrakhan goes on to ridicule the virgin birth of Jesus by teaching that since Allah was a man, he had sexual intercourse with Mary to produce Jesus.

On Mankind

Elijah continued Fard's racism by teaching that the black race was the first and the last, the creator of the universe, and the origin of all other races. Black people were actually gods.

On the other hand, white people were not created by Allah. An evil black scientist by the name of YaKub made the white man out of his dark side.

YaKub spent six hundred years creating him. Thus white people are devils and not really human beings at all.

An Obvious Contradiction

There is an obvious contradiction between the teaching that white people are intrinsically evil and the teaching that a white man by the name of Wallace D. Fard was Allah incarnate.

Another contradiction which should be pointed out is that if a black scientist/god by the name of YaKub made the white man, then why blame the white man for being evil?

If YaKub really existed and did what Elijah claimed, then isn't the black man the author of evil? We have yet to receive a rational response to these contradictions.

Death and the Afterlife

Using Jehovah's Witness theology, Elijah Muhammad denied that people went to heaven or hell at death. He taught the Watchtower concept of "soul sleep."

Like the Witnesses, black Muslims deny that there is a hell in the afterlife but teach that "hell" is here on earth.

On the End of the World

Following the Watchtower literature which proclaimed 1914 as the "beginning of the end," Elijah Muhammad twisted it to mean that 1914 signaled the end of the white man's rule and the beginning of black power.

Elijah went on to prophesy that Allah would personally intervene in the 1970's by destroying the white man and putting black people in control of the world. This fit in with the teaching of the Jehovah's Witnesses who were proclaiming 1975 as the end of the world.

The obvious failure of Allah to intervene in 1975 as predicted by Elijah is a tremendous embarrassment to black Muslims today. This false prophecy totally destroys any attempt to view him as a prophet.

Farrakhan and Armageddon

The present black Muslim leader, Louis Farrakhan, has publicly predicted that Armageddon is near. According to him, the giant UFO "wheel" will soon destroy the white man.

Malcolm X

The other serious embarrassment of the black Muslim movement in America was the murder of Malcolm X.

The son of another black Baptist pastor, Malcolm Little converted to the teachings of Elijah Muhammad. Elijah himself changed Little's name to that of Malcolm X.

After 12 years of devoted service to the Nation of Islam, Malcolm woke up to Elijah's many moral problems, such as his 13 illegitimate children, his greed and jealousy, and the constant strife which filled Elijah Muhammad's life.

These things began to bother him. How could Elijah be from Allah and do all the evil things he did?

It was during his pilgrimage to Mecca that for the first time he clearly saw the heretical and racist nature of the black Muslim movement in America. They were not Muslims at all. The whole thing was a sham.

Malcolm X Speaks Out

After much soul searching, Malcolm publicly renounced the teachings of W.D. Fard and Elijah Muhammad and began to warn the black community about the racist and heretical nature of the Nation of Islam. He also warned people that he might be murdered for his courageous stand.

This action by someone so well known in the movement and in the black community at large could not be overlooked. A black Muslim death squad assassinated Malcolm X in a public dance hall on February 22, 1965.

But the damage had already been done. The movement fell apart and has fractured into many warring sects.

Elijah's Death

Elijah Muhammad died in 1975. Since that time black Muslims have claimed that he is actually alive and that he is the Christ and the Savior! They even held a "Savior's Day" celebration in honor of Elijah Muhammad, Fard, and Farrakhan.

They are now claiming that Elijah Muhammad did the miracles of Christ such as healing the sick and raising the dead. Of course, not one of these miracles has ever been documented.

Louis Farrakhan

Under Louis Farrakhan's flamboyant leadership, the Nation of Islam movement is growing and prospering today. As Allah in human form, his will and word are absolute.

The stated goal of the movement is to set up a separate "Nation of Islam" complete with its own military and justice system.

Terrorist Money

The main mosque in South Chicago has been renovated through a large gift of money from Libyan dictator

Khadafy, a known sponsor of terrorism throughout the world.

The financial bonding of Farrakhan to Khadafy is potentially dangerous by anyone's standard. Is it any wonder that Farrakhan followed Khadafy in publicly supporting Saddam Hussein during the Gulf War?

Killing for Islam

In a videotape of the 1991 "Savior's Day" celebration, the head of Farrakhan's "army" stated that he was tired of hearing people say that they were willing to die for Islam.

What he wanted to know was if they were willing to *kill* for Islam. The time is coming, he said, when they must kill all that is white that is not right.

During this celebration, Farrakhan acknowledged that when he went to Mecca the black Muslim movement in America was condemned as heretical by orthodox Islam. But this did not seem to bother him in the least.

Conclusion

What was the legacy of Elijah Muhammad? It was one of deception, fraud, racism, greed, immorality, and murder.

He did not raise the black man to new heights or give him the dignity he needed. Elijah's attempt to fight white racism with black racism only compounded the problem.

And his rejection of the gospel was actually the rejection of the only way for all people regardless of color to find true dignity.

It must be viewed as just one more indigenous American cult like the Jehovah's Witnesses or the Mormons.

Chapter 11 Bibliography

Clayborne Carson, *Malcolm X: The F.B.I. File* (Carroll & Graf Pub., N.Y., 1991).

James H. Cone, *Martin and Malcolm and America* (Orbis Books, Maryknoll, N.Y., 1991).

Mustafa El-Amin, *The Religion of Islam and the Nation of Islam: What Is the Difference?* (El-Amin Productions, Newark, New Jersey, 1990).

Carl F. Ellis Jr., *Beyond Liberation* (InterVarsity Press, Downers Grove, 1983).

E.U. Essien-Udom, *Black Nationalism* (Dell, New York, 1962).

Peter Goldman, *The Death and Life of Malcolm X* (Harper & Row, New York, 1974).

C. Eric Lincoln, *The Black Muslim in America* (Beacon Press, Boston, 1973).

Elijah Muhammad, *The Message to the black Man in America* (Muhammad Mosque, Chicago, 1965).

———, *Supreme Wisdom* (Muhammad Mosque, Chicago, n.d.).

Malcolm X, *Autobiography of Malcolm X,* (Grove Press, New York, 1964).

Bruce Perry, *Malcolm: The Life of the Man Who Changed Black America* (Station Hill, Barryton, N.Y., 1991).

APPENDICES
NOTES
BIBLIOGRAPHY

An Analysis
of the Hadith

Introduction

While most people understand that the "Bible" of the Muslims is called the Quran, they do not generally know that the religion of Islam has other sacred writings which are viewed by Muslims as being just as inspired and authoritative as the Quran.

This other Islamic "Bible" is called the Hadith. It is a collection of early Muslim traditions which record the words and deeds of Muhammad according to his wives, family members, friends and Muslim leaders which are not usually found in the Quran.

The Inspired Hadith

The Muslim scholar, Dr. Muhammad Hamidullah, in his book, *Introduction to Islam*, states that "the custodian and repository of the original teachings of Islam" are found "above all in the Quran and the Hadith" (p. 250). To this he adds that "the Quran and the Hadith" are "the basis of all [Islamic] law" (p. 163).

The reason according to Dr. Hamidullah that Muslims revere the Hadith as well as the Quran is that the Hadith is as divinely inspired as the Quran itself!

> The teachings of Islam are based primarily on the Quran and the Hadith, and, as we shall presently see, both are based on divine inspiration (p. 23).

This is why Muslim writers such as Hammudullah Abdalatati in his book, *Islam In Focus* (The Muslim Converts' Association of Singapore, Singapore, 1991), state that the Hadith is "considered the Second Source of Islam" because,

> all the articles of faith . . . are based upon and derived from the teachings of the Quran and the Traditions [Hadith] of Muhammad (p. 21).

Thus it is no surprise to find that the material in the Hadith is considered inspired and authoritative to orthodox Muslims.

The Translation We Will Use

We are using the nine-volume translation of the Hadith made by Dr. Muhammad Muhsin Khan entitled, *The Translation of the Meaning of Sahih Al-Bukhari* (Kazi Publications, Lahore, Pakistan, 1979).

It is recommended and approved by all Muslim authorities, including the spiritual heads of Mecca and Medina.

Based Upon Al-Bukhari

Dr. Khan's work is a faithful translation of the Hadith put together by none other than the greatest of all Hadith scholars, Al-Bukhari.

The introduction states:

> It has been unanimously agreed that Iman Bukhari's work is the most authentic of all the other works in Hadith literature put together. The authenticity of Al-Bukhari's work is such that the religious learned scholars of Islam said concerning him: "The most authentic book after the Book of Allah [i.e., the Quran] is Sahih-Al-Bukhari" (p. xiv).
>
> He only chose approximately 7275 [Hadiths] of which there is no doubt about their authenticity.
>
> [Allah] revealed to him the Glorious Quran and the Second Inspiration, i.e., his Traditions.
>
> It is incumbent upon you to strive hard to do righteous deeds according to the traditions of Muhammad as is clearly expressed in his Hadith (p. xvii).

Dr. Khan does not hesitate to describe the Hadith as "the Second Inspiration" and to state that it is "incumbent" upon every Muslim to believe and to obey it.

The Muslim Dilemma

The reason that we went to such lengths to prove the highest religious authorities of Islam view the Hadith as being inspired and authoritative is that many Muslims will deny this when confronted with some of the obviously absurd teachings of Muhammad.

In one radio program, one Muslim caller argued in a circle as follows:

> Muhammad was Allah's prophet. Therefore he could not have said something so stupid as to suggest that we should drink camel urine. Thus you are a liar, Dr. Morey. The Hadith cannot say this.

After I went on to prove from the Hadith that Muhammad did indeed recommend camel urine, he responded:

> We Muslims only recognize the Holy Quran as God's Book. We do not accept the Hadith as inspired.

Of course, he had to deny the inspiration of the Hadith in order to avoid having to defend Muhammad on the drinking of urine.

We understand the dilemma of modern Muslims. While they desperately want to maintain that Muhammad was Allah's apostle, yet the Hadith clearly reveals that Muhammad could not be inspired because he taught many things which are not only patently wrong but absurd.

The Final Straw

To the Western mind, the material found in the Hadith is the proverbial final straw that breaks the camel's back! If Muhammad was truly a prophet and an apostle, then Muslims must defend the indefensible.

Pre-Islamic Information

The Hadith gives us much material concerning pre-Islamic Arabia which is not found in the Quran. For example, in Hadith no. 658, vol. 3 and in vol. 5, Hadith no. 583, we are told that there were 360 idols at the Kabah when Muhammad conquered it.

This bit of information is not mentioned in the Quran. Yet, this information provides us with important clues as to religious practices in pre-Islamic times.

Ritualism

The Hadith contains the intricate details of just how and in what way various Islamic religious rituals and laws are to be carried out.

A detailed analysis of the entire nine volumes of the Hadith will give the English reader a concise summary of the extra-quronic words and works of Muhammad.

The Origins of Islamic Rituals

It is thus with great delight that we offer our summary of the Hadith to Western readers who have wondered about the origins of some of the rituals and laws of Islam which seem so strange to them. Many of these "strange" rituals actually come from the Hadith and not from the Quran.

The Driving Force

The driving force behind the Hadith is the all-consuming question, "What must I do to be forgiven by Allah and to be admitted to paradise?"

In the Hadith, Muhammad does not give us vague generalities. He tells the reader exactly what to do, how to do it, and in what order to do it.

For example, Muhammad lays down very specific rules about how, where, and in what way to urinate. Whether or not you follow these urination rules determines whether or not you end up in hellfire or paradise.

The Working Assumption

The working assumption throughout the Hadith is that without Allah's forgiveness, no one may enter into Paradise. Hellfire awaits those who do not gain Allah's favor.

But to gain Allah's acceptance and forgiveness is no easy manner. One must EARN Allah's forgiveness by following an elaborate set of rules and rituals. One mistake can cancel out all that you have done up to that point. There is no concept of salvation by grace in the Hadith.

The Hadith sets forth the rules and rituals which must be followed to earn salvation. Those Muslims who ignore these rules and rituals imperil their immortal souls.

With these brief words, we will now begin a summary of the contents of the Hadith.

Section I
Muhammad as a Man

The Hadith reveals much about the man Muhammad that we do not find recorded in the Quran. This is important because Muslims want us to believe that he was Allah's apostle.

Thus Muhammad's character as a man is crucial. Was Muhammad the kind of man we should follow? The Hadith supplies us with the crucial information about his personality and character that we need in order to make an intelligent and informed decision.

A White Man

First, as to his race, the Hadith clearly states that Muhammad was a white man. This is stated so many times in so many ways that it is quite obvious that the authors of the Hadith were deeply concerned less someone think that Muhammad was a black man. Hence the emphasis on the whiteness of Muhammad.

This will come as quite a shock to the "Black Muslims" who have claimed that "Islam is a black man's religion" because "Muhammad was a black man."

Since Muhammad was a white man, then the Nation of Islam is a "white man's religion"!

Muhammad, a White Devil?

In numerous radio debates with Black Muslims, they have expressed great surprise to learn that the Hadith clearly states that Muhammad was a white man. But since they pay lip service to the inspiration of the Hadith, in the end, they had to submit to its authority.

Indeed, if "All white men are devils" as Elijah Muhammad and Louis Farrakhan have claimed, then Muhammad as well as Wallace Fard was a white devil!

Jesus, a White Devil?

The Hadith even claims that Muhammad saw Jesus in a dream and that Jesus was a white man with straight hair (vol. 9, Hadith no. 242).

The Black Muslims will not be happy with this Hadith either. This means that Jesus was a white devil too!

The Hadithic Evidence

In vol. 1, Hadith no. 63, we read,

> While we were sitting with the Prophet in the Mosque, a man came riding on a camel. He made his camel kneel down in the Mosque, tied its foreleg and then said, "Who amongst you is Muhammad?" At that time the Prophet was sitting amongst us [his companions] leaning on his arm. We replied, "This white man reclining on his arm." The man then addressed him, "O Son of 'Abdul Muttalib."

The Hadith in vol. 2, no. 122, refers to Muhammad as "a white person." And in vol. 2, no. 141, we are told that when Muhammad raised his arms, "the whiteness of his armpits became visible."

If the above passages are not clear enough, we are later told in vol. 1, no. 367 that Anas "saw the whiteness of the penis of Allah's Prophet."

Black People—Raisin Heads

As to the attitude of Muhammad about black people, he referred to them as "raisin heads" in vol. 1, no. 662 and vol. 9, no. 256.

Throughout the Hadith, black people are referred to as slaves.

If this is not insulting enough to black people, Muhammad felt that if someone dreamed of a black woman, she was an evil omen of a coming epidemic of disease (vol. 9, nos. 162, 163).

Muhammad: A Slave Owner!

In Hadith no. 435, vol. 6, when Umar bin Al-Khattab came to the home of Muhammad, he found that,

> a black slave of Allah's apostle was sitting on the first
> step.

From this and other references in the Hadith, it is clear that Muhammad was a slave master and that he owned black slaves. As a matter of fact, in almost every instance in which black people are mentioned in the Hadith, they were the personal slaves of Muhammad! This was in stark contrast to Jesus of Nazareth who did not own slaves but came to set men free.

Short Tempered

Second, in terms of Muhammad's personality, he was short-tempered and easily angered.

When Muhammad heard of someone leading in prolonged prayers, the Hadith records,

> I never saw the prophet more furious in giving advice
> than he was on that day (vol. 1, no. 90).

Since he claimed to be a "prophet," a man asked Muhammad where to find his lost camel. The Hadith records that,

> The Prophet got angry and his cheeks or his face
> became red (vol. 1, no. 91).

He Did Not Like Questions

Muhammad did not actually like anyone to ask him questions about his claims to prophethood or revelation. He went so far as to say,

> Allah has hated you... [for] asking too many ques-
> tions (vol. 2. no. 555; vol. 3, no. 591).

Even when he was asked questions, the Hadith records,

> The Prophet was asked about things which he did not
> like, when the questioner insisted, the Prophet got
> angry (vol. 1, no. 92).

When those who asked questions "saw the [anger] on the face of the Prophet," they often withdrew their questions (vol. 1, no. 92).

But this did not please Muhammad either. When the people rightfully complained that he wanted them to accept what he said with no questions asked,

> The Prophet told them repeatedly [in anger] to ask him anything they liked (vol. 1, no. 30).

But the people had learned not to ask anything.

No Sense of Humor

Third, Muhammad did not have a sense of humor. He did not permit anyone to joke about him or his doctrines.

In vol. 2, no. 173, the Hadith tells the story of one elderly man who watched Muhammad and his disciples bowing and touching their foreheads to the dirt while reciting Surat-an-Najm. (The early Muslims prided themselves on their dirty foreheads and looked down on all other forms of prayer.)

When the old man saw their foreheads becoming dirty, as a joke, he picked up some dirt and put it to his own forehead and said, "This is sufficient for me."

The old man was saying that if the important thing was to get dirt on your forehead when you pray, then it would be a lot easier to pick up some dirt and smear it on your forehead. Ha! Ha!

Obviously, the old man's joke was directed against the Muslim pride over their dirty foreheads.

But Muhammad was not amused by the old man or his joke. The Hadith records that the Muslims murdered the old man in cold blood!

Bitter and Vengeful

Fourth, Muhammad was a bitter, vengeful man who had numerous people murdered when they got on his bad side.

While Muhammad told others not to kill people when in Mecca and, in particular, not to kill people at the Kabah, when Muhammad heard that Ibn Khatal was taking refuge in the Kabah, he said, "Kill him." He was dragged out and butchered (vol. 3, no. 72).

One particularly horrifying example of Muhammad's blood lust is found in vol. 3, no. 687 of the Hadith.

Allah's Prophet said, "Who will kill Ka'b bin Al-Ash-
raf as he has harmed Allah and his Apostle?" Muhammad bin Maslama [got up and] said, "I will kill
him." They [Muhammad bin Maslama and his com-
panions] came to him as promised and murdered
him. Then they went to the Prophet and told him.

Tribal Conflict

Muhammad's demand that somebody murder for him sometimes caused problems among the tribes. On one occasion, when
Aisha was only 15 years old, she was accused of adultery.

According to her story as the Hadith records it in vol. 3, no.
829, she had accidently left her necklace behind when she went to
answer the call of nature.

When she went back to find it, the caravan went on without
her. They did not realize that she had not rejoined them.

Later a Muslim by the name of Safwan bib Mu'attal As-Su-
lami Adh-Dhakwani found her and on his own camel brought her
back to the caravan.

A Nasty Rumor

This started the nasty rumor that she was having an affair
with Safwan. The entire Muslim community was in an uproar about
the issue.

According to Aisha, the leader of those who accused her was
named 'Abdullah bin Ubai bin Salul. His followers spread forged
statements of false accusers about her adultery.

Aisha returned to be with her parents while Muhammad,

> called upon 'Ali bin Abu Talib and Usama bin Zaid...
> to consult them about divorcing his wife [i.e., Aisha].

They counseled him not to divorce Aisha on the basis of mere
rumors but to ask Aisha's woman servant Buraira if she had ever
seen anything suspicious about her.

> Buraira said, "No, by Allah who has sent you with the
> truth, I have never seen in her anything faulty except
> that she is a girl of immature age, who sometimes
> sleeps and leaves the dough for the goats to eat."

The footnote in the Hadith points out that Aisha was only 15 years old at the time. According to the Hadith, Aisha had been only 6 years old when Muhammad married her! He consummated the marriage when she was only 9 years old!

A Request for Murder

With Buraira's word that Aisha was innocent,

> Allah's Prophet ascended the pulpit and requested that somebody support him in punishing 'Abdullah bin Ubai bin Salul. Allah's Prophet said, "Who will support me to punish that person who has hurt me by slandering the reputation of my family?" Sa'd bin Mu'adh got up and said, "O Allah's Apostle! By Allah, I will relieve you from him. If that man is from the tribe of the Anus, then we will chop his head off, and if he is from our brothers, the Khazraj, then order us, and we will fulfill your order."

The chief of the Khazraj, Sa'd bib 'Ubada, jumped up to defend his tribe and said, "You cannot kill him." This in turn led Sa'd bin Mu'adh to say, "By Allah, we will kill him."

The entire situation got out of control and the Anus tribe and the Khazraj tribe prepared to fight each other over the issue. It took some time for Muhammad to get things quieted down.

Muhammad took the easiest way out and claimed to have received a special revelation from Allah that Aisha was innocent.

Thus the issue for Muslims was now settled because Allah had spoken. Those infidels who would dare question Allah's apostle on this issue would meet the fate of all infidels.

Muhammad Was Not Innocent

Fifth, according to the Hadith, Muhammad was a sinner in need of forgiveness. He was NOT sinless as Islam now claims. When Muhammad was asked by Abu Huraira,

> What do you say in the pause between Takbir and recitation? Muhammad replied, I say, "O Allah, set me apart from my sins as the East and West are set apart from each other and clean me from sins as a

white garment is cleaned of dirt [after thorough washing]. O Allah! Wash off my sins with water, snow and hail" (vol. 1, no. 711).

In Hadith no. 319, vol. 8, Abu Huraira said,

I heard Allah's Apostle saying, "By Allah! I ask for forgiveness from Allah and turn to him in repentance more than seventy times a day."

Muhammad's wife Aisha records that the early Muslims did not regard Muhammad as sinless.

They said, "O Allah's Prophet! We are not like you. Allah has forgiven your past and future sins" (vol. 1, no. 19).

This Hadith is clear that Muhammad's disciples praised him because his sins were forgiven and not because he did not have any sins to forgive.

It goes on to say in Hadith no. 781, vol. 1:

The Prophet used to say frequently in his bowings and prostrations, "O Allah! Our Lord! All praises are for You. O Allah! Forgive me."

In Hadith no. 375, the men of Quraish repeatedly said,

May Allah forgive his Apostle!

Obviously, these men did not view Muhammad as sinless!

The same can be said of a group of three men who discussed in Hadith no. 1, vol. 7, that Allah had forgiven Muhammad of his sins.

In vol. 5, no. 724, Aisha said that she heard Muhammad pray,

O Allah! Forgive me and bestow your mercy on me.

During his supposed night journey through seven heavens, Jesus says concerning Muhammad,

Muhammad, the Slave of Allah, whose past and future sins were forgiven by Allah (vol. 6, no. 3).

Appendix A

In Hadith no. 494, vol. 6, Muhammad is commanded by Allah to ask for forgiveness for his sins.

Abu Musa heard Muhammad pray this prayer,

> O my Lord! Forgive my sins and my ignorance. Forgive my sins of the past and of the future which I did openly or secretly (vol. 8, no. 407).

The only one not "touched" (i.e., corrupted) by Satan at birth was Jesus according to Muhammad in Hadith no. 506, vol. 4. Thus Muhammad was himself "touched" by Satan.

The sins of Muhammad included torturing people by cutting off their hands and feet and burning out their eyes with hot irons (vol. 1, no. 234); leaving them to bleed to death after cutting off their limbs (vol. 8, nos. 794, 795); making people die of thirst (vol. 8, no. 796).

Sixth, Muhammad was superstitious.

Muhammad believed in the power of the "evil eye" and told people to recite the Quran to fight it (vol. 7, no. 636).

He also believed in good and bad omens such as the appearance of certain birds and other animals (vol. 4, nos. 110, 111; vol. 7, nos. 648, 649, 650).

Muhammad was even afraid that evil spirits might enter his body whenever he urinated or defecated. Thus he prayed for special protection (vol. 1, no. 144).

He was also afraid of a strong wind.

> Narrated Anas: Whenever a strong wind blew, anxiety appeared on the face on the Prophet [fearing that the wind might be a sign of Allah's wrath] (vol. 2, no. 144).

When a solar or lunar eclipse took place, Muhammad was seized with fear that the Day of Judgment had arrived.

> The sun eclipsed and the Prophet got up, being afraid that it might be the Hour [i.e., Day of Judgment]. Then he said, "These signs which Allah sends do not occur because of the life or death of somebody, but Allah makes his worshippers afraid by them. So when you see anything thereof, proceed to remember Allah, invoke him and ask for forgiveness" (vol. 2, no. 167).

Perhaps nowhere else does Muhammad's superstitious nature come out than in his worship of the black stone found at the Kabah in
Mecca. That he kissed and adored it is plainly stated in vol. 2, no. 667.

Muhammad believed that if you placed a green palm leaf on the grave of those suffering in that grave, their pain would be lessened as it dried (vol. 2, no. 443).

He was superstitious about even numbers. He always avoided them. Thus he stipulated that an odd number of stones be used in cleaning oneself after defecating.

> Whoever cleans his private parts with stones should
> do it with odd number of stones (vol. 1, no. 162).

People could turn into rats, monkeys, and pigs according to Muhammad. In particular, he claimed that the Jews were transformed into rats! (vol. 4, nos. 524, 569, and chap. 32).

In Hadith 660, vol. 7, we read that,

> Magic was working on Allah's Apostle so that he used
> to think he had had sexual relations with his wives
> while he actually had not.

To prove the depth of Muhammad's belief in and fear of magic, one need only read from Hadith no. 656 to no. 664 in vol. 7.

He Dyed His Hair Red

Seventh, Muhammad dyed his hair an orangish red color.

> Narrated 'Ubaid Ibn Juraij: And about the dyeing of
> hair with Henna; no doubt I saw Allah's Prophet
> dyeing his hair with it and that is why I like to dye
> [my hair with it] (vol. 1, no. 167).

After Muhammad died, some of his red hair was kept and shown to others (vol. 4, no. 747; vol. 7, no. 785).

But He Had Lice

While he kept his hair from growing white by dying it red, he failed to keep it free of lice (vol. 9, no. 130).

Muhammad's Sexual Appetite

Eight, Muhammad's sexual activities were legendary. His harem had over 20 women in it. The Hadith makes the claim that he was able to have sex with all of them every day before prayers. He supposedly had the sexual strength of 30 men!

Such claims were made to impress the Arabs who at that time believed that ceaseless sexual activity was paradise.

> Narrated Qatada: Anas bin Malik said, "The Prophet used to visit all his wives in a round, during the day and the night and they were eleven in number." I asked Anas, "Had the Prophet strength for it?" Anas replied, "We used to say that the Prophet was given the strength of thirty [men]" (vol. 1, no. 268).
>
> Aisha said, "I scented Allah's prophet and he went round [had sexual relation with] all his wives" (vol. 1, no. 270 and no. 267).

See also vol. 7, nos. 5, 6, and 142 which state the same thing.

As to how many wives the prophet had, we are told by Anas bib Malik in vol. 1, no. 268 that "they were eleven in number." He would often choose new sexual partners from the women captured during his conquests. (See vol. 1, no. 367 as an example.)

In flat contradiction, Hadith no. 142, vol. 7, says that Muhammad had only nine wives.

Women devotees would also offer themselves to be in Muhammad's harem.

> A woman came to Allah's Prophet and said, "O Allah's Apostle! I want to give myself to you" (vol. 3, no. 505.A.).

Muhammad would look at the women who offered themselves as sexual partners and if they were beautiful enough, they were allowed to enter his harem.

But if they did not meet his approval, they were "given" to other men. The woman who was given by Muhammad to someone else evidently had no choice in the matter. See also vol. 7, no. 24 where a woman offers her sexual favors to Muhammad.

In addition to wives and devotees, Muhammad had sex with the slave girls which were either given to him or he purchased (vol. 7, nos. 22, 23).

Section II
Muhammad as a Prophet
The "Seal of Prophethood"

Perhaps the most amazing passage in the Hadith is where the claim is made that Muhammad was a prophet because he had a fatty tumor on his neck between his shoulders!

> Narrated As-Sa'ib bin Yazid: I stood behind him and saw the seal of Prophethood between his shoulders, and it was like the "Zir-al-Hijla" [meaning the button of a small tent, but some say "egg of a partridge"] (vol. 1, no. 189; see also vol. 4, no. 741).

This Hadith is remarkable because it reveals the Arabs believed that the "seal of prophethood" was a physical lump between the shoulders!

A Pagan Shaman

Muhammad was a shaman who controlled the jinn, i.e., the spirits who lived in the rocks, water, and trees (vol. 1, no. 740; vol. 5, no. 199).

Physical Signs of Revelation

It is in the Hadith that we find a full description of what physically happened to Muhammad when he supposedly received his revelations "strongly, frequently and regularly."

As we have already pointed out, these are the characteristics of someone who has epilepsy or some other brain disorder. Let the reader decide for himself.

The Hadithic Evidence

1. Muhammad would experience ringing in his ears as if he were hearing bells: vol. 1, no. 1; vol. 4, no. 438.
2. His heart would beat rapidly: vol. 1, no. 3.
3. His face would turn red: vol. 2, chap. 16, p. 354; vol. 5, no. 618; vol. 6, no. 508.
4. He would breathe heavily: vol. 6, no. 508.

5. He would sometimes suddenly fall down or lie down: vol. 2, chap. 16, p. 354; vol. 4, no. 461, "I fell on the ground"; vol. 5, no. 170, "he fell down unconscious on the ground with both his eyes [open] towards the sky"; vol. 6, no. 448, "I fell down upon the ground."

6. He would ask to be covered with a sheet or blanket: vol. 1, no. 3; vol. 2, chap. 16, p. 354; vol. 3, no. 17; vol. 4, no. 461, "I fell on the ground...and said, "Cover me! [with] a blanket, cover me!" Then Allah sent a revelation: "O, You wrapped up in a blanket!" vol. 5, no. 170, "He fell down unconscious on the ground with both his eyes [open] towards the sky. When he came to his senses, he said, 'My waist sheet! My waist sheet!'" (vol. 6, nos. 447, 448, 468, 481).

7. His lips would tremble as he lay on the ground: vol. 1, no. 4.

8. He heard and saw things no else heard or saw: vol. 1, nos. 2, 3; vol. 4, nos. 458, 461; vol. 6, no. 447.

9. He would sweat profusely: vol. 1, no. 2; vol. 2, no. 544; vol. 3, no. 829; vol. 4, no. 95; vol. 5, no. 462.

10. He would sometimes snore like a camel: vol. 2. chap. 16, p. 354; vol. 3, no. 17.

11. He would sometimes dream: vol. 1, no. 3; vol. 5, no. 659; vol. 6, no. 478.

Section III
The Miracles of Muhammad

There are no recorded miracles of Muhammad in the Quran. We already documented from the Quran that Muhammad denied that he did any miracles except for the Quran.

But after his death, Muhammad's disciples began to invent miracles for him because they had to escape the stigma that their prophet was inferior to the miracles of Moses, Jesus, and the pagan soothsayers.

What is so amazing about some of these pretended miracles is that they were often originally performed by Moses, Jesus, and pagan magicians but now transferred to the prophet!

One gets the distinct impression that when a Jew or a Christian pointed out some miracle recorded in the Bible, the Muslims replied, "Then our prophet Muhammad must have done that too."

The following is a summary of the miracles of Muhammad found in the Hadith. There are a few other miracles mentioned in connection with the early Muslims such as talking wolves and palm trees preaching Islam, but since they do not involve Muhammad directly, they do not concern us.

I. The Moon Cut in Half

When the Meccans asked Muhammad to do a miracle to prove that he was Allah's prophet, he supposedly reached up with his sword and cut the moon in half.

> vol. 4, nos. 830, 831, 832
> vol. 5, nos. 208, 209, 210, 211
> vol. 6, nos. 387, 388, 389, 390

How and by whom the two sides of the moon were joined together is not told. That would be an even greater miracle to us!

This so-called miracle means that either Muhammad had a very BIG sword or that the moon was very SMALL.

Historically, the Arabs at that time believed that the sun and the moon were the size they appeared to the human eye. Thus the moon was about the size of a basketball. Muhammad evidently had no problem cutting in half such a small moon.

This "miracle" is very doubtful for if the Meccans had seen Muhammad cut the moon in half, why did he have to conquer them by military force? Would not such a glorious miracle convert them?

II. A Cry Baby Palm Tree

A palm tree cried like a baby because Muhammad used a pulpit to preach instead of standing beneath the tree to preach. Muhammad left his pulpit and caressed the trunk of the tree until it stopped crying.

> vol. 2, no. 41
> vol. 4, no. 783

III. Water in the Wilderness

On one occasion when the Muslims needed water, Muhammad called for a bowl. Then he made water flow out of his fingernails into the bowl until everyone had all the water they needed.

> vol. 1, nos. 170, 194
> vol. 4, nos. 773, 774, 775, 776, 779

How many people drank that water? One Hadith says 70 (vol. 4, no. 774). Another Hadith says 80 (vol. 4, no. 775). Yet another Hadith says around 300 hundred (vol. 4, no. 772). But then others say 1500 hundred (vol. 4, no. 776 and vol. 5, no. 473).

Two things are demonstrated from the conflicting numbers of 70, 80, 300, and 1500. The Hadiths often contradict each other and the miracles of Muhammad got bigger and better each time they were told!

IV. *Multiplying Bread*

Muhammad fed the multitudes by multiplying the bread just like Jesus. He even had then come up in groups of ten to further mimic the miracle of Jesus.

vol. 4, nos. 778, 781

V. *Shouting Foods*

Food would shout out loud and glorify Allah as Muhammad ate it. The picture of someone calmly eating talking bread and meat is incredible.

vol. 4, no. 779

VI. *The Open Grave*

When a man who had once been a Muslim and then reconverted back to Christianity died and was buried, the earth would not accept his body but threw it out of the grave. This was a supposed miracle of Muhammad.

vol. 4, no. 814

VII. *Multiplying Dates*

Muhammad multiplied several heaps of dates to cover the debt of a Muslim.

vol. 4, no. 780

VIII. *Muhammad's Chest Split Open*

Gabriel opened Muhammad's chest and washed his insides with Zam-zam water. He took wisdom and faith and poured them into his chest and then closed it up.

vol. 1, no. 345

IX. *The Night Journey*

The night journey of Muhammad to Jerusalem and then through seven heavens where he talked with Adam, Idris, Moses, Jesus, and Abraham is considered by some to be the greatest miracle of Muhammad surpassed only by the Quran itself.

vol. 1, nos. 211, 345

X. *Memories in a Sheet*

Muhammad enabled one of his followers to remember the Hadiths by having the man take off his sheet and lay it on the ground. Then Muhammad went through the motion of picking something up and then scooping it into the sheet. He then told the man to put his sheet back on and the man never forgot anything after that.

> vol. 1, no. 119
> vol. 4, no. 841

XI. A Rain Maker

When a drought threatened the people, they went to Muhammad and asked him to pray to Allah for rain. After he prayed, it rained.

> vol. 2, no. 55

XII. A Drought Maker

When the tribes of Mudar refused to accept Muhammad as Allah's prophet, he cursed them in prayer that drought and famine would destroy them for seven years. Within a year the people were reduced to eating hides, carcasses, and rotten dead animals.

> vol. 2, nos. 120, 121

XIII. A Prophecy of Wind

Muhammad was able to predict that a strong wind was going to blow. He warned people to prepare for it. One man who did not heed his warning was blown away to a mountain called Taiy.

> vol. 2, no. 559

XIV. A Prophecy on Dates

Muhammad was able to estimate the number of dates a garden would contain before it was harvested.

> vol. 2, no. 559

XV. Healing the Eyes with Spit

Muhammad cured a man with eye trouble by spitting in his eyes. The man never had eye trouble after that.

> vol. 4, no. 192
> vol. 5, no. 51

All manner of diseases could be cured by Muhammad's spit according to Hadiths no. 641 and 642, vol. 7.

XVI. His Spit Becomes Water

When Muhammad spit into a dry well, it filled with enough water to satisfy 1400 hundred men and their camels.

> vol. 4, no. 777
> vol. 5, nos. 471, 472

XVII. Multiplied Water

Muhammad multiplied the water in two water skins to satisfy all the people and yet the skins were more full at the end than at the beginning.

> vol. 4, no. 771

XVIII. Miracles by Rubbing

Muhammad healed a broken leg by rubbing it.

> vol. 5, no. 371

XIX. Healings Through Recitation

Snake bites, scorpion stings, and all kinds of illnesses were healed by Muhammad by waving his hand over the wound, reciting of the Quran, and the applying of his spit to the wound.

> vol. 7, nos. 637, 638, 639, 640, 641, 642

XX. Dream Interpretation

Muhammad would interpret the dreams of others as well as his own dreams. He claimed that the dream of a Muslim is "one of the forty-six parts of prophetism." Thus he was involved in the occult art of dream interpretation.

> vol. 2, no. 468
> vol. 9, nos. 111-171

Conclusions

Some of these miracles are clearly copied from the miracles of Moses (ex. III), Jesus (ex. IV, XVI) and pagan prophets (ex. IX). The rest reflect the occultic practices prevalent in Muhammad's day (ex. XIX).

Section IV
On Jihad (Holy War)

The Hadith reveals that Muhammad wanted his religion to be spread primarily by the sword. It is filled with commands to make war upon non-Muslims in order to force them to embrace Islam.

Jihad was so important to Muhammad that he made it the second most important deed in Islam.

> Allah's apostle was asked, "What is the best deed?" He replied, "To believe in Allah and his Apostle." The questioner then asked, "What is the next [in goodness]?" He replied, "To participate in Jihad [religious fighting] in Allah's cause" (vol. 1, no. 25).

Anas bin Malik recorded that,

> Allah's Apostle vanquished them by force and their warriors were killed; their children and women were taken as captives. Safiya was taken by Dihya Al-Kalbi and later she belonged to the Allah's Apostle who married her (vol. 2, no. 68).

A brief summary on Muhammad's teachings on Jihad should be informative to Westerners.

The translator of the Hadith, Dr. Muhammad Muhsin Khan, wrote an introduction to the Hadith which included a discourse on the subject of Jihad by Sheikh Abdullah bin Muhammad bin Hamid, Sacred Mosque of Meccah, Saudi Arabia (vol. 1, pgs. xxii-xl).

This is the most frank Muslim discussion of Jihad we have ever read. It does not deny or play down Muhammad's demand that Muslims must force Jews, Christians, and pagans to either embrace Islam or submit to political and financial suppression. Indeed, it tries to stimulate and motivate Muslims to engage in Jihad today.

According to Sheikh Abdulla bin Muhammad bin Hamid, Muhammad,

> commanded the Muslims to fight against all the pagans as well as against the people of the scriptures [Jews and Christians] if they do not embrace Islam, until they pay the Jizya [a tax levied on the Jews and the Christians who do not embrace Islam] (p. xxiv).

Jihad thus employs several different methods:

1. There is the Jihad of the sword.

People are to be either converted or subdued through the violence of military force (vol. 1, p. xxii). Chapter 19 of the Hadith speaks of those who convert to Islam,

> by compulsion or for fear of being killed (vol. 1, p. 27).

Muhammad said,

> I have been ordered to fight against the people until they testify that none has the right to be worshipped but Allah and that Muhammad is Allah's Prophet, and offer prayers and give obligatory charity, so if they perform all that, then they save their lives and property (vol. 1, no. 24).

This is why Muhammad warned the King of the Byzantines,

> If you become a Muslim you will be safe (vol. 1, no. 6).

If the king did not convert, he and his kingdom would be destroyed and enslaved.

The Hadith records how Mecca was conquered by force to Islam in vol. 1, no. 104.

In vol. 3, no. 495, we read,

> Allah made the Prophet wealthy through conquests.

When a Muslim murdered someone during a Jihad, he got to take the man's property.

> The Prophet said, "Whoever has killed an enemy and has proof of that, will possess his spoils" (vol. 4, no. 370).

This is the driving force behind Muslim violence in Africa today. In such countries as Nigeria and Sudan, hundreds of thousands of Christians and pagans have been brutally slaughtered or enslaved in the name of Jihad because they would not convert to Islam.

> Our Prophet, the Messenger of our Lord, has ordered us to fight you till you worship Allah alone or give Jizya (vol. 4, no. 386).

2. There is the Jihad of taxation.

Those who refuse to embrace Islam must pay a special tax called Al-Jizya (vol. 4, chap. 21, pgs. 251-252). This financial burden suppresses non-Muslims and makes their life as hard as possible.

3. There is the Jihad of financial reward.

In Iraq, a free university education has been offered to any Christian or Jew who will embrace Islam. A "bounty" of one thousand dollars has been offered to any South African black who will renounce Christianity and embrace Islam. They will also be paid $500 for any other blacks they convert to Islam.

It has been quite common to tell Americans and Europeans that if they want to continue to work in the oil business in Saudi Arabia, they must convert to Islam. No church is allowed to be built on Saudi soil in the attempt to suppress Christian worship.

4. There is the Jihad of fear.

The death penalty is applied to anyone who renounces Islam and embraces another religion such as Christianity. As this book goes to print, there are Christians being tortured in prison in Egypt whose only "crime" was to convert to Christianity.

5. There is the Jihad of slavery.

The only place in the world where black chattel slavery is practiced today is in Muslim countries. The London Economist (1/6/90) reported that the Sudanese Muslims are presently capturing and then selling black women and children of the Dinka Christian Tribe for as little as $15 a head!

Even the U.N. released a report on slavery that points out that the Muslims are still enslaving blacks. This has also been pointed out in the May 4, 1992 special edition of *Newsweek* on slavery.

Non-Muslim women who go to Saudi Arabia to work as maids are often enslaved by their Muslim employers, beaten, and raped at will. When they try to escape, the Saudi government will not let them leave the country but returns them to their masters.

6. The Jihad of the courts.

Non-Muslims are denied equal access to and equal protection before the law because their testimony in court is not valid against a Muslim (vol. 3, chap. 31, pgs. 525-526). This applies even to murder!

> No Muslim should be killed for killing an infidel (vol. 4, no. 283; vol. 9, no. 50).

7. There is a Jihad after death.

A Muslim is "to fight on [Muhammad's] behalf in his lifetime and after his death" (vol. 1, chapter 43).

8. There is the Jihad of Paradise.

Any Muslim who is killed while fighting in a Jihad will go straight to the sexual pleasures of Paradise (vol. 1, no. 35; vol. 4, no. 386).

Section V
On the Quran and the Hadith

The Quran was written in heaven according to Hadith no. 643, vol. 9. Thus no earthly pre-Islamic sources for the material found in the Quran should exist. But they do exist in great abundance.

Thus it is no surprise to find that the Quran was written in the Quraish dialect (vol. 6, no. 507). This fact is often not known by non-Arab Muslims.

The Quran after Muhammad's death was scattered on palm leaves, rocks, bones, etc. (vol. 6, no. 509). Thus the Hadith itself bears witness to the fact that Muhammad did not prepare a manuscript of the Quran before his death.

As a matter of record, the Hadith confirms that the Quran was put together by the Caliph Uthman after Muhammad died. This point is often denied by those Muslims who are ignorant of their own scriptures.

> Uthman got the Quran compiled and sent a few of its copies to far off places (vol. 1, no. 63). Uthman... wrote the manuscripts of the Holy Quran in the form of a book (vol. 4, no. 709).

See also vol. 6, nos. 507 and 510.

When Uthman finished his version of the Quran, the Hadith records that he tried to destroy all the conflicting Qurans (vol. 6, no. 510). This is clear proof that there were conflicting versions of the Quran.

The fact that the Quran is missing certain verses and that other verses were abrogated is admitted in the Hadith in vol. 4, nos. 57, 62, 69, 299; vol. 6, nos. 510, 511.

The Hadith even records that when certain people died, those portions of the Quran known only to them perished with them (vol. 6, no. 509).

The Hadith records that Muhammad at times was bewitched and said and saw things under satanic inspiration (vol. 4, nos. 400, 490).

This admission on the part of the Hadith destroys in principle the Muslim claim that Muhammad was infallibly inspired.

Since it is admitted that Muhammad at times did and said things under satanic inspiration, then this in principle calls into question everything he did and said.

Like the Quran, the Hadith puts speeches into the mouths of biblical characters such as Noah, Moses, Jesus, etc., which they could not have spoken because of the vocabulary used, the doctrines taught, the historical references made, etc. They are clearly fraudulent.

> vol. 1, chap. 1, p. 16
> vol. 1, nos. 74, 78, 124

The Hadith admits that it has variant readings and contradictory Hadiths (vol. 1, nos. 42, 47, 74, 78, 80, 81, 86, 102, 107, 112, 159, 160, 161; vol. 3, nos. 159-161).

The translator admits in a footnote in vol. 3, no. 159,

> Hadith No. 159 contradicts the Hadith of Al-Hassan.

Like the Quran, some Hadiths were canceled or abrogated: vol. 1, nos. 179, 180.

Section VI
On Apostasy

The Hadith makes the repeated claim that no one ever leaves Islam.

> He then asked, "Does anybody amongst those who embrace his [i.e., Muhammad's] religion become displeased and renounce the religion afterwards?" I replied, "NO" (vol. 1, nos. 6 and 48).

Then it contradicts itself by saying that death is the punishment for those who leave.

> The Prophet said, "If somebody [a muslim] discard his religion [of Islam], kill him" (vol. 4, no. 260).

It even records the murders of those who left Islam for another religion (vol. 5, no. 630).

Volume nine of the Hadith has an entire section dedicated to warning those who would leave Islam—that they will be murdered (see vol. 9, pgs. 10-11, 26, 45-50, 341-342).

> So, wherever you find them, kill them, for whoever kills them shall have reward on the Day of Resurrection (vol. 9, no. 64).

Section VII
On Jews and Christians

Muhammad taught that the Jews worshiped Ezra as the Son of Allah just as Christians worshiped Jesus as the Son of Allah (vol. 1, p. xvii). He was wrong on both counts.

Muhammad said,

> Any Jews or Christians who heard about me and did not believe in me and what was revealed to me of the Holy Quran and my traditions, his ultimate destination is the [Hell] Fire (vol. 1, p. li.).

According to Hadith no. 414, vol. 2, Muhammad said,

> Allah cursed the Jews and the Christians because they took the graves of their Prophets as places for worship.

Section VIII
Muhammad on Women

Muhammad taught that the majority of the people in hell were women!

> The Prophet said, "I was shown the Hell-fire and that the majority of its dwellers were women" (vol. 1, nos. 28, 301; vol. 2, no. 161).

The reason the majority of the people in hell were women is stated in vol. 2, no. 541,

> O Women! I have not seen anyone more deficient in intelligence and religion than you.

Muhammad believed that women were "deficient in intelligence" and thus they should not be given equal rights under Islamic law.

For example, he legislated that a woman's testimony in court was worth only half that of a man. Thus it would take the testimony of two women to offset the testimony of one man. Imagine what this would do to women who were raped!

> The Prophet said, "Isn't the witness of a woman equal to half of that of a man?" The women said, "Yes." He said, "This is because of the deficiency of a woman's mind" (vol. 3, no. 826).

Muhammad even ruled that women are to receive only half of what their brothers receive in inheritance (vol. 4, no. 10). Thus women are financially punished for being females.

Perhaps the most degrading picture of women is that Paradise will have beautiful women, whose only purpose is to satisfy the sexual urges of men, chained to different corners.

> The statement of Allah, Beautiful women restrained [i.e., chained] in pavilions. Allah's Apostle said, "In Paradise there is a pavilion made of a single hollow pearl sixty miles wide, in each corner there are wives who will not see those in the other corners; and the believers will visit and enjoy them."

Section IX
On Urine and Feces

Muhammad had a psychological obsession with urine and feces. In fact, he spent a great deal of time teaching on where, when, and how to urinate and defecate.

He was so obsessed with the subject that he taught that if someone got urine on his clothes or body, they suffered hellfire in the afterlife!

> One of the major sins is not to protect oneself [one's clothes and body] from one's urine [i.e., from being soiled with it]. Once the Prophet, while passing one of the grave-yards of Medina or Mecca, heard the voices of two persons being tortured in their graves.

> The Prophet then added, "Yes! [they are being tortured for a major sin]. Indeed, one of them never saved himself from being soiled with his urine" (vol. 1, chap. 57, no. 215).

According to vol. 2, no. 443, Muhammad said that people are tortured in hellfire because they soil themselves with urine.

Yet, at the same time, Muhammad ordered people to drink camel urine mixed in milk as medicine!

> So the Prophet ordered them to go to the herd of camels and to drink their milk and urine [as a medicine] (vol. 1, no. 234).

The rules for urination and defecation are as follows:
1. You must not face Mecca when urinating or defecating (vol. 1, nos. 146, 147, 150, 151).
2. You must not use your right hand to hold or wipe yourself (vol. 1, nos. 155, 156).
3. You must wash your privates after going to the bathroom (vol. 1, nos. 152, 153, 154, 157).

Section X
Muhammad's Believe or Not

Muhammad taught many things which seem to the modern reader to be patently absurd. Some of his beliefs were so far out that no one today could possibly accept or defend them. Yet, we recognize that sincere Muslims must do so or give up their claim that he was Allah's Apostle.

We understand their difficulty. How can they defend the indefensible? How can they justify what is so obviously absurd? This is the crux of the matter.

The following teachings of Muhammad are a partial list of some of the strange things he taught to his disciples.

I. The Colossus Adam

In Hadith no. 543, vol. 4, we read,

> The Prophet said, "Allah created Adam, making him 60 cubits tall."

This would make Adam around 90 ft. tall! Was Adam really as tall as a three-story building? How tall was Eve? And their children?

And why are we not that tall? How could he stand if he were that heavy? Does not the science of human anatomy tell us that Adam could not have been 60 cubits tall? What Muslim is prepared to defend Muhammad's 90 ft. Adam?

II. *The Fly in the Cup*

If a fly falls into your cup, do not worry about it because Muhammad said that while one wing has the disease, the other has the antidote. So drink up (vol. 4, no. 537).

III. *No Dogs Allowed*

Angels will not enter a house if a dog is there according to vol. 4, no. 539. Thus Hadith no. 540, vol. 4, reads,

> Allah's Apostle ordered that the dogs should be killed.

Dog lovers would not make good Muslims.

IV. *Islamic Genetics*

Muhammad claimed that Gabriel gave him the secret as to why a child looks like its father or its mother. This answer was given to prove that Muhammad was Allah's Apostle.

He declared,

> As for the resemblance of the child to its parents: If a man has sexual intercourse with his wife and gets a discharge first, the child will resemble the father, and if the woman gets her discharge first, the child will resemble her (vol. 4, no. 546).

What modern Muslim is prepared to prove that one's "discharge" and not genetics is the key to the physical characteristics of one's children?

V. *Stars as Missiles*

The stars were created by Allah as missiles to throw at the devils, according to Muhammad in vol. 4, chap. 3, p. 282. Astronomers should be interested in this doctrine of Muhammad.

VI. Do as I Say—Not as I Do

Muhammad commanded everyone to have a will when he himself failed to make one.

> I asked Adullah bin Abu Aufa, "Did the Prophet make a will?" He replied, "No." I asked him, "How is it then that the making of a will has been enjoined on people?" (vol. 4, nos. 3, 4).

VII. What Do Spirits Eat?

The jinn or spirits eat dung and bones according to Muhammad (vol. 5, no. 200)! This bit of information is as far out as one can go.

VIII. No Assurance

Muhammad had no assurance of salvation.

> The Prophet said, "By Allah, though I am the Apostle of Allah, yet I do not know what Allah will do to me" (vol. 5, no. 266).

IX. Murder and Deceit

Muhammad agreed to the murder of a man through lies and deceit (vol. 5, no. 369). He evidently did not believe in the sanctity of truth or life.

X. Six Hundred Wings

The angel Gabriel has 600 wings according to Muhammad (vol. 6, no. 380).

XI. Satan in Your Nose

Muhammad would suck in water up his nose and then blow it out because,

> Satan stays in the upper part of the nose all night (vol. 4, no. 516).

I have yet to find a single Muslim who will defend this strange doctrine and practice of Muhammad.

XII. Fevers from Hell

Muhammad believed that a fever when sick was from the heat of hell.

> The Prophet said, "Fever is from the heat of the [Hell] fire, so cool it with water" (vol. 4, nos. 483-486).

All sorts of questions come to mind when you really think about this doctrine of Muhammad.

XIII. Noah's Ark

Noah's Ark appeared and floated in front of their eyes (vol. 6, no. 391, chap. 288). How or why this happened we are not told.

XIV. Dirty Water Magic

Muhammad's followers fought over who would get the dirty water left over from his washings. They would smear it on their bodies or drink it to secure a magical blessing from it (vol. 1, nos. 187, 188).

XV. Holy Spit

Even more gross was the practice of Muhammad spitting into the hands of his followers so they could smear his saliva on their faces!

> By Allah, whenever Allah's Apostle spitted, the spittle would fall in the hand of one of them [i.e., the Prophet's companions] who would rub it on his face and skin (vol. 3, no. 891).

It was in this light that we can understand why Muhammad smeared dead bodies with his spit (vol. 2, nos. 360, 433).

XVI. Satan Urinating in the Ears

Satan urinates into the ears of those who fall asleep during prayers (vol. 2, no. 245).

XVII. Passing Wind

According to Muhammad, if you commit the sin of "hadath" (the passing of wind through the anus) while you are engaged in prayer, Allah will not hear your prayers! (vol. 1, no. 628; vol. 9, no. 86). Why Allah would be offended by the natural smells of the human body escapes us.

XVIII. Bad Breath

Bad breath means that Allah will not hear your prayers. You may not eat garlic or onions before going to prayers because Allah will not hear you with their smell on your breath. (vol. 1, nos. 812, 813, 814, 815; vol. 7, nos. 362, 363).

XIX. Yawning Is from Hell

Yawning is from Satan according to Muhammad in Hadith no. 509, vol. 4.

It seems clear from this Hadith, and the two previous ones, that it was really Muhammad who was offended by such things as bad breath, yawning, or passing wind.

That God would be offended by the natural processes of the human body which He made is not acceptable to the rational mind.

XX. Green Birds

According to Sheikh Abdullah bin Muhammad bin Hamid of the Sacred Mosque of Mecca (Saudi Arabia),

> Allah's Apostle said: The souls of the martyrs are in the bodies of green birds dwelling in paradise wherever they like (vol. 1, p. xxviii).

If this is true, we do not understand how these "green birds" will be able to "enjoy" all those beautiful women chained in different corners of paradise!

Conclusions

If Muhammad was truly Allah's apostle, then what he taught came from Allah and must be true.

But if what he said is so outlandish and absurd that it cannot be true, then how can he be an apostle of Allah?

The logic is inescapable. The Hadith is the final blow that explodes the claim of Muhammad that he was an apostle and prophet of God.

APPENDIX B

English Translations of the Quran

The Muslim claim that the Arabic of the Quran cannot be translated into English or any other language has led to the absurdity of non-Arab Muslims praying and reciting Arabic prayers and verses without having a clue as to what they are saying!

It is also an insult to an entire generation of Arabic scholars who have had no difficulty in translating the Quran.

The first English translation of the Quran by Western scholars was by George Sale in 1734.

This was not done again until 1861 by Rodwell. Palmer followed in 1880, Wherry in 1882, Pickthal in 1930, Arberry in 1955, Mercier in 1956, and Dawood in 1974.

Muslim translations of the Quran into English began with Adul Hakim Khan in 1905. Mirza Hairat's translation followed in 1919.

The Ahmadiya sect produced one in 1915. Yusuf Ali's translation came out in 1934 and Rashad Khalifa's in 1981.

Since so many English-speaking Muslims in the West use Ali's translation, we have followed the numbering of verses which he adopted.

This may cause some confusion, since the Quran did not originally have numbered verses. Numbering the verses is a Western idea.

Translators differ somewhat in how they number the verses. What is verse 5 in Yusuf Ali's translation may be verse 4 in Pickthal.

Arberry does not even number each verse; he numbers paragraphs instead.

If you are looking up a verse reference we have given in this book and you are not using Ali's translation, then look before and after the verse we indicate and you will find it.

We have pointed out earlier that such Muslim translators as Yusuf Ali will not hesitate to mistranslate the Arabic text in order to keep the English writer from discovering obvious errors in the Quran. Ali is first of all an apologist for Islam, and then a translator.

But Ali does serve a purpose that he never imagined: By his constant footnotes in which he tries to rescue the Quran from its many errors and contradictions, he unwittingly alerts the reader to the presence of these errors and contradictions in the text.

Also, his irrational arguments and his obvious mistranslations of various texts (such as the one on the Trinity), lead the reader to become highly suspicious that Ali is desperately trying to hide something. The readers of his translation must be aware of its hidden apologetic agenda.

APPENDIX C

The Moon God and Archeology

As we've learned, the religion of Islam has as its focus of worship a deity named "Allah." The Muslims claim that Allah in pre-Islamic times was the biblical God of the patriarchs, prophets, and apostles.[1] The issue here is thus one of *continuity*.

The Muslim's claim of continuity is essential to their attempt to convert Jews and Christians. If "Allah" is part of the flow of divine revelation in Scripture, then it is the next step in biblical religion. Thus we should all become Muslims. But, on the other hand, if Allah was a pre-Islamic pagan deity, then its core claim is refuted.

Religious claims often fall due to the results of hard sciences such as archeology. So, instead of endlessly speculating about the past, we can look to science to see what the evidence reveals. As we shall see, the hard evidence demonstrates that the god Allah was a pagan deity. In fact, he was the moon god who was married to the sun goddess and the stars were his daughters.

Archeologists have uncovered temples to the moon god throughout the Middle East. From the mountains of Turkey to the banks of the Nile, the most widespread religion of the ancient world was the worship of the moon god.

Late Assyrian or Neo-Babylonian Seal.
Baltimore, Walters Art Gallery

The Sumerians, in the first literate civilization, left thousands of clay tablets describing their religious beliefs. As demonstrated by Sjoberg and Hall, the ancient Sumerians worshiped a moon god who was called many different names. The most popular names were Nanna, Suen, and Asimbabbar.[2] His

symbol was the crescent moon. Given the amount of artifacts concerning the worship of this moon god, it is clear that this was the dominant religion in Sumeria.

The cult of the moon god was the most popular religion throughout ancient Mesopotamia. The Assyrians, Babylonians, and Akkadians took the word *Suen* and transformed it into the word *Sin* as their favorite name for this deity.[3] As Professor Potts pointed out, "Sin is a name essentially Sumerian in origin which had been borrowed by the Semites."[4]

The Babylonian Moon-god

In ancient Syria and Canna, the moon god Sin was usually represented by the moon in its crescent phase. At times, the full moon was placed inside the crescent moon to emphasize all the phases of the moon. The sun goddess was the wife of Sin and the stars were their daughters. For example, Istar was a daughter of Sin.[5]

Stele from Amrit,
Phoenicia Paris, Louvre

Sacrifices to the moon god are described in the Ras Shamra texts. In the Ugaritic texts, the moon god was sometimes called Kusuh. In Persia, as well as in Egypt, the moon god is depicted on wall murals and on the heads of statues. He was the judge of men and gods.

As a matter of fact, everywhere in the ancient world the symbol of the crescent moon can be found on seal impressions, steles, pottery, amulets, clay tablets, cylinders, weights, earrings, necklaces, wall murals, and so on. In Tell-el-Obeid, a copper calf was found with a crescent moon on its forehead. An idol with the body of a bull and the head of a man has a crescent moon inlaid on its forehead with shells. In Ur, the Stela of Ur-Nammu has the crescent symbol placed at the top of the register of gods because the moon god was the head of the gods. Even bread was baked in the form of a crescent as an act of devotion to the moon god.[6]

The Ur of the Chaldees was so devoted to the moon god that it was sometimes called Nannar in tablets from that time period. A temple of the moon god has been excavated in Ur by Sir Leonard Woolley. He dug up many exmaples of moon worship that are now displayed in the British Museum. Harran was likewise noted for its devotion to the moon god.

In the 1950's a major temple to the moon god was excavated at Hazor in Palestine (see Map 1). Two idols of the moon god were found. Each was a statue of a man sitting upon a throne with a crescent moon carved on his chest (see Diagram 1). The accompanying inscriptions make it clear that these were idols of the moon god (see Diagrams 2 and 3). Several smaller statues were also found which were identified by their inscriptions as the daughters of the moon god (see Diagram 4).[7]

What about Arabia? As pointed out by Professor Coon, "Muslims are notori-

Stele from Ras Shamra, North Syria

ously loath to preserve traditions of earlier paganism and like to garble what pre-Islamic history they permit to survive in anachronistic terms."[8]

During the nineteenth century, Arnaud, Halevy, and Glaser went to southern Arabia and dug up thousands of Sabean, Minaean, and Qatabanian inscriptions which were subsequently translated (see Map 2). In the 1940's, archeologists G. Caton Thompson and Carleton S. Coon made some amazing discoveries in Arabia. During the 1950's, Wendell Phillips, W.F. Albright, Richard Bower, and others excavated sites Qataban, Timna, and Marib (the ancient capital of Sheba).

An Egyptian monolith

Diagram #1
The Moon-god from all four sides. Note the crescent moon carved on his chest.
Two such idols were found at the site.

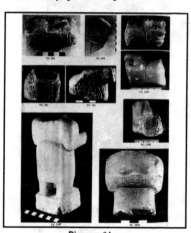

Diagram #2
Note the Moon-god idol on the left and the worship
tablets in front of the altar lying flat on the ground.

Diagram #3
A worship tablet, arms
outstretched toward the Moon-
god here represented by the full
moon within the crescent moon.

Diagram #4
Pieces of the idols of the daughters of the Moon-god.
The inscription identifies them as "daughters of god."

Thousands of inscriptions from walls and rocks in northern Arabia have also been collected. Reliefs and votive bowls used in worship of the "daughters of Allah" have also been discovered. The three daughters, Al-Lat, Al-Uzza, and Manat are sometimes depicted together with Allah the moon god represented by a crescent moon above them.[9]

The archeological evidence demonstrates that the dominant religion of Arabia was the cult of the moon god. The Old Testament constantly rebuked the worship of the moon god (see, for example: Deuteronomy 4:19; 17:3; 2 Kings 21:3,5; 23:5; Jeremiah 8:2; 19:13; Zephaniah 1:5). When Israel fell into idolatry, it was usually to the cult of the moon god. In Old Testament times, Nabonidus (555–539 B.C.), the last king of Babylon, built Tayma, Arabia, as a center of moon god worship. Segall stated, "South Arabia's stellar religion has always been dominated by the Moon-god in various variations."[10] Many scholars have also noticed that the moon god's name, "Sin," is a part of such Arabic words as "Sinai," the "wilderness of Sin," and so forth.

When the popularity of the moon god waned elsewhere, the Arabs remained true to their conviction that the moon god was the greatest of all gods. While they worshiped 360 gods at the Kabah in Mecca, the moon god was the chief deity. Mecca was in fact built as a shrine for the moon god. This is what made it the most sacred site of Arabian paganism.

In 1944, G. Caton Thompson revealed in her book *The Tombs and Moon Temple of Hureidha*, that she had uncovered a temple of the moon god in southern Arabia (see Map 3). The symbols of the crescent moon and no less than 21 inscriptions with the name Sin were found in this temple (see Diagram 5).[11] An idol which may be the moon god himself was also discovered (see Diagram 6). This was later confirmed by other well-known archeologists.[12]

The evidence reveals that the temple of the moon god was active even in the Christian area. Evidence gathered from both North and South Arabia demonstrate that moon-god worship was clearly active even in Muhammad's day and was still the dominant cult.

According to numerous inscriptions, while the name of the moon god was Sin, his title was al-ilah, "the deity," meaning that he was the chief or high god among the gods. As Coon pointed out, "The God Il or Ilah was originally a phase of the Moon God."[13]

The moon god was called al-ilah, the god, which was shortened to Allah in pre-Islamic times. The pagan Arabs even used Allah in the names they gave to their children. For example, both Muhammad's father and uncle had Allah as part of their names. The fact

Diagram #5
Arabian Moon Temple—
The name of the Moon-god is carved into stone.

Diagram #6
Arabian Moon Temple—An idol of the Moon-god

that they were given such names by their parents proves that Allah was the title for the moon god even in Muhammad's day. Professor Coon says, "Similarly, under Mohammed's tutelage, the relatively anonymous Ilah, became Al-Ilah, The God, or Allah, the Supreme Being."[14]

This fact answers the questions: "Why is Allah never defined in the Quran?" and "Why did Muhammad assume that the pagan Arabs already knew who Allah was?"

Muhammad was raised in the religion of the moon god Allah. But he went one step further than his fellow pagan Arabs. While they believed that Allah (the moon god) was the *greatest* of all gods and the supreme deity in a pantheon of deities, Muhammad decided that Allah was not only the greatest god but the *only* god.

In effect he said, "Look, you already believe that the moon god Allah is the greatest of all gods. All I want you to do is to accept the idea that he is the *only* god. I am not taking away the Allah you already worship. I am only taking away his wife and his daughters and all the other gods."

This is seen from the fact that the first point of the Muslim creed is not "Allah is great" but "Allah is the greatest"—he is the greatest among the gods. Why would Muhammad say that Allah is the "greatest" except in a polytheistic context? The Arabic word is used to contrast the greater from the lesser.

That this is true is seen from the fact that the pagan Arabs *never* accused Muhammad of preaching a *different* Allah than the one they already worshiped. This "Allah" was the moon god according to the archeological evidence.

Muhammad thus attempted to have it both ways. To the pagans, he said that he still believed in the moon god Allah. To the Jews and the Christians he said that Allah was their God, too. But both the Jews and the Christians knew better and they rejected his god Allah as a false god.

Al-Kindi, one of the early Christian apologists against Islam, pointed out that Islam and its god Allah did not come from the Bible but from the paganism of the Sabeans. They did not worship the God of the Bible but the moon god and his daughters al-Uzza, al-Lat, and Manat.[15]

Dr. Newman concludes his study of the early Christian-Muslim debates by stating, "Islam proved itself to be ... a separate and antagonistic religion which had sprung up from idolatry."[16] Islamic scholar Caesar Farah concluded, "There is no reason, therefore, to accept the idea that Allah passed to the Muslims from the Christians and Jews."[17]

The Arabs worshiped the moon god as a supreme deity. But this was *not* biblical monotheism. While the moon god was greater than all other gods and goddesses, this was still a polytheistic pantheon of deities. Now that we have the actual idols of the moon god,

Islamic Mosque in Columbia, Missouri

it is no longer possible to avoid the fact that Allah was a pagan god in pre-Islamic times.

Is it any wonder then that the symbol of Islam is the crescent moon? That a crescent moon sits on top of their mosques and minarets? That a crescent moon is found on the flags of Islamic nations? That the Muslims fast during the month which begins and ends with the appearance of the crescent moon in the sky?

Conclusion

The pagan Arabs worshiped the moon god Allah by praying toward Mecca several times a day; making a pilgrimage to Mecca; running around the temple of the moon god called the Kabah; kissing the black stone; killing an animal in sacrifice to the moon god; throwing stones at the devil; fasting for the month that begins and ends with the crescent moon; giving alms to the poor; and so on.

The Muslim's claim that Allah is the God of the Bible and that Islam arose from the religion of the prophets and apostles is refuted by solid, overwhelming archeological evidence. Islam is nothing more than a revival of the ancient moon god cult. It has taken the symbols, the rites, the ceremonies, and even the name of its god from the ancient pagan religion of the moon god. As such, it is sheer idolatry and must be rejected by all those who follow the Torah and Gospel.

MAPS

The Temple of the Moon-god at Hazor

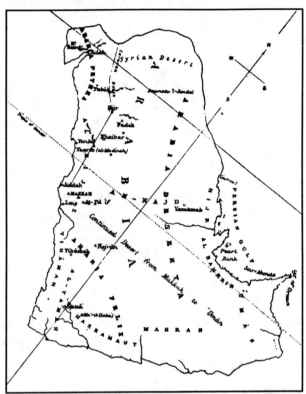

A map of the Arabian Peninsula during the time of Prophet Muhammad

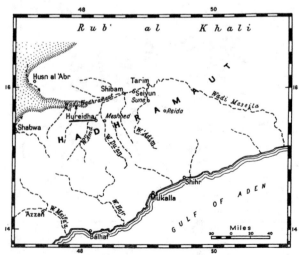

The site of the moon-temple in southern Arabia

Notes

Introduction

1. For estimates of 3 to 4 million Muslims in the United States, see Victor Khalil and Deborah Khalil, "When Muslims Meet Christians," in *Christian Herald*, July/Aug. 1988, p. 45; Kent Hart, "Da'wah and the Koran: Islam in America," in *Eternity*, vol. 39, 1988, no. 3, pp. 5ff.; "Islam in America," in *U.S. News & World Report*, Oct. 8, 1990; Mimi Hall, "Arab Americans Speak Out," in *USA Today*, Feb. 6, 1991, p. 1.
2. The program aired on Feb. 22, 1991, on radio station WHP in Harrisburg, PA.
3. The 1989 *Information Please Almanac* (Boston: Houghton Mifflin Company, 1989), p. 400.
4. A good example of Muslim anti-Christian literature would be Maurice Bucaille's book *The Bible, The Quran and Science* (Indianapolis: American Trust Pub., 1979).

Chapter 2—The Key to Islam

1. Arthur J. Arberry, *Religion in the Middle East* (London: Cambridge University Press, 1969), II:3.
2. Kerry Lovering, "Mecca Challenges the World," in *Africa Now*, Sudan Interior Mission, Jan./Feb. 1979 p. 39.
3. Victor Khalil and Deborah Khalil, "When Muslims Meet Christians," *Christian Herald*, July/Aug. 1988, p. 43.
4. *The Concise Dictionary of Islam*, ed. Cyril Classe (London: Stacey Inter., 1989), p. 179.
5. John McClintock and James Strong, *Cyclopedia of Biblical, Theological, and Ecclesiastical Literature* (Grand Rapids: Baker Book House, 1981 reprint), I:339.
6. *The Encyclopedia of Islam*, eds. Gibb, Levi-Provencial, Schacht (Leiden: J. Brill, 1913), I:543-47.
7. Thomas Hughes, *A Dictionary of Islam* (London: Allen & Co., 1885), pp. 18ff.
8. J.A. Thompson, *The Bible and Archeology* (Grand Rapids: Wm. B. Eerdmans Pub. Co., 1965), pp. 13-36.
9. Quoted in the *Harrisburg Patriot News*, Feb. 6, 1991, p. A-3.
10. Ali Dashti, *23 Years: A Study of the Prophetic Career of Mohammad* (London: George Allen & Unwin, 1985), pp. 33-38.
11. Ibid., p. 113.
12. Ibid., p. 113.
13. Ibid., p. 114.
14. Ibid., p. 56.

Chapter 3—Pre-Islamic Arabia

1. M. Bravmann, *The Spiritual Background of Early Islam* (Leiden: E.J. Brill, 1972).
2. Jane Smith, *An Historical and Semitic Study of the Term Islam as Seen in a Sequence of Quran Commentaries* (University of Montana Press, for Harvard University Dissertations, 1970).
3. William Montgomery Watt, *Muhammad's Mecca* (Edinburgh: Edinburgh University Press, 1988), pp. 18-19.
4. For the fullest account of this group, see Marshall Hodgson, *The Order of Assassins* (Gravenhage: Mouton & Co., 1955).
5. *Chamber's Encyclopedia* (London: International Learning Center, 1973), IX:453.

6. *Praeger Encyclopedia of Art* (New York: Praeger, 1971), pp. 68-70. *Encyclopedia of World Art* (New York: McGraw-Hill Book Co., 1959), I:537ff.

7. *Encyclopedia Britannica*, 15:150ff.

8. Besides the standard references to "jinn" in Islamic dictionaries and encyclopedias, see Dashti and Bravmann for two particularly enlightening discussions.

9. Nearly all Western reference works have a section on the pre-Islamic history of Mecca, the Kabah, and the black stone. For example, see the *Encyclopedia Britannica*, 15:150ff.; *Encyclopedia of Religion* (ed. Eliade), 8:225ff.; *International Standard Bible Encyclopedia*, I:218.

10. For further information on the Sabeans, see *Encyclopedia of Religion* (ed. Eliade), 1:364-365; 7:303; 8:225ff.

11. This is common knowledge and supported by all general reference works such as *Encyclopedia Britannica* and all standard encyclopedias and dictionaries on Islam.

12. Michael Nazar-Ali, *Islam: A Christian Perspective* (Philadelphia: Westminster Press, 1983), p. 21.

13. Alfred Guillaume, *Islam* (London: Penguin Books, 1954), p. 6.

14. Augustus H. Strong, *Systematic Theology* (Valley Forge: Judson Press, 1976 reprint), p. 186.

Chapter 4—The Cult of the Moon God

1. H.A.R. Gibb, *Mohammedanism: An Historical Survey* (New York: Mentor Books, 1955), p. 38.

2. Arthur Jeffery, ed., *Islam: Muhammad and His Religion* (New York: The Liberal Arts Press, 1958), p. 85.

3. For an interesting discussion of the origins of *allah*, see J. Blau, "Arabic Lexiographical Miscellanies," *Journal of Semitic Studies*, vol. XVII, no. 2, 1972, pp. 173-190. That *allah* is an Arabic word is also pointed out in Hastings' *Encyclopedia of Religion and Ethics*, I:326.

4. *Encyclopedia of Religion and Ethics*, ed. James Hastings (Edinburgh: T. & T. Clark, 1908), I:326.

5. *Encyclopedia of Religion*, eds. Paul Meagher, Thomas O'Brian, Consuela Aherne (Washington D.C.: Corpus Pub., 1979), I:117.

6. *Encyclopedia Britannica*, I:643.

7. *Encyclopedia of Islam*, eds. Houtsma, Arnold, Basset, Hartman (Leiden: E.J. Brill, 1913), I:302.

8. *Encyclopedia of Islam* (ed. Gibb), I:406.

9. *Encyclopedia of Islam*, eds. Lewis, Menage, Pellat, Schacht (Leiden: E.J. Brill, 1971), III:1093.

10. *The Facts on File: Encyclopedia of World Mythology and Legend,* ed. Anthony Mercatante (New York, The Facts on File, 1983), I:41.

11. *Encyclopedia of Religion and Ethics* (ed. Hastings), I:326.

12. Henry Preserved Smith, *The Bible and Islam: or, The Influence of the Old and New Testament on the Religion of Mohammed* (New York: Charles Scribner's Sons, 1897), p. 102.

13. Kenneth Cragg, *The Call of the Minaret* (New York: Oxford University Press, 1956), p. 31.

14. William Montgomery Watt, *Muhammad's Mecca*, p. vii. See also his article, "Belief in a High God in Pre-Islamic Mecca," *Journal of Semitic Studies*, vol. 16, 1971, pp. 35-40.

15. Caesar Farah, *Islam: Beliefs and Observations* (New York: Barrons, 1987), p. 28.

16. E.M. Wherry, *A Comprehensive Commentary on the Quran* (Osnabruck: Otto Zeller Verlag, 1973), p. 36.

17. Guillaume, *Islam*, p. 7.
18. *Encyclopedia of World Mythology and Legend*, I:61.

Chapter 5—Allah and the God of the Bible

1. Samuel Zwemer, *The Muslim Doctrines of God: An Essay on the Character of Allah According to the Koran* (New York: American Tract Society, 1905).
2. Samuel Schlorff, "Theological and Apologetical Dimensions of Muslim Evangelism," *Westminster Theological Journal*, vol. 42, no. 2 (Spring 1980), p. 338.
3. For the Christian view of God, see H. Spencer, *Islam and the Gospel of God* (Madras: S.P.C.K., 1956) and Augustus Strong, *Systematic Theology*, p. 186. For the Muslim viewpoint, see Mohammad Zia Ullah, *Islamic Concept of God* (London: Kegan Paul Inter., 1984).
4. Quoted in Zwemer, *Muslim Doctrines*, p. 21.
5. *International Standard Bible Encyclopedia* (ed. Orr), II:1323.

Chapter 6—The Life of Muhammad

1. Dozens of such biographies, Muslim and Western, are listed in the bibliography.
2. Alfred Guillaume, *Islam*, pp. 24-25.
3. John McClintock and James Strong, *Cyclopedia of Biblical, Theological, and Ecclesiastical Literature* (Grand Rapids: Baker Book House, 1981 reprint), 6:406.
4. Hurgronji, *Mohammedanism* (Westport, CT: Hyperion Press, 1981), p. 46.
5. McClintock and Strong, *Cyclopedia*, 6:406. For further documentation of such symptoms as falling to the ground, profuse sweating, odd noises, etc., see Pfander, *The Balance of Truth*, pp. 343-348.
6. For a full treatment of this contradiction, see W. Montgomery Watt, *Muhammad's Mecca*, pp. 54-68.
7. For a Muslim apologetical work aimed at overturning nearly every point raised by Western scholarship, see Muhammad Husayn Haykal's book, *The Life of Muhammad* (Delhi: Crescent Pub., 1976). His book is marred by the constant use of circular reasoning and by an utter lack of any scholarship. For detailed discussions by Western scholars see Guillaume, Watt, Gibb, Jeffery, etc.
8. W. Montgomery Watt, *Muhammad's Mecca*, pp. 70-72, 86-93.
9. See Guillaume, *Islam*, pp. 37-38.
10. Ali Dashti, *23 Years*, p. 86.
11. Ibid., p. 87.
12. *Encyclopedia Britannica*, 15:648.
13. For Muslim documentation, see Ali Dashti, *23 Years*, pp. 88-91. For Western scholars, see Alfred Guillaume, *Islam*, pp. 47-48.
14. Dashti, *23 Years*, pp. 120-138.

Chapter 7—Muhammad and Jesus Christ

1. Muslims have cited such passages as Genesis 49:10; Deuteronomy 18:15-18; 32:21; 33:2; Psalm 45; 149; Isaiah 21:7 and others. For detailed Western responses to these claims, see C. Pfander, *The Balance of Truth* (London: The Religious Tract Society, 1910), pp. 228ff., 252ff. John Gilchrist, *Is Muhammed Foretold in the Bible?* (Benoni, South Africa: *Jesus to the Muslims*, 1987). See also the article by Percy Smith, "Did Jesus Foretell Ahmed?" *Muslim World*, vol. 12 (1922), pp. 71ff.
2. Guillaume, *The Traditions of Islam* (London: Clarendon Press, 1924), p. 138.
3. Ali Dashti, *23 Years*, p. 1.
4. Ibid., p. 38.
5. Ibid., p. 3.
6. Guillaume, *Traditions*, p. 133.
7. Ibid., pp. 134-135.

224

Chapter 8—The Structure of the Quran

1. Quoted by Professor H.A. Gibb in *Mohammedanism, An Historical Survey*, p. 37.
2. Salmon Reinach, *Orpheus: A history of Religion* (New York: Livercraft, Inc., 1932) p. 176.
3. Edward Gibbon, *The Decline and Fall of the Roman Empire* (London: Milman Co., n.d.) I:365.
4. McClintock and Strong, *Cyclopedia*, V:151
5. Dashti, *23 Years*, p. 28.
6. *Concise Encyclopedia of Islam*, p. 231.
7. Ibid., p. 230. See also Guillaume, *Islam*, p. 57.
8. Abdullah Mandudi, *The Meaning of the Quran* (Lahore: Islamic Pub. ltd., 1967), p. 17.
9. Ibid., p. 17.
10. Dashti, *23 Years*, p. 28.

Chapter 9—Muslim Claims for the Quran

1. *Shorter Encyclopedia of Islam*, p. 276.
2. Dashti, *23 Years*, p. 48.
3. Ibid., p. 50.
4. Arthur Jeffery, *The Foreign Vocabulary of the Quran* (Baroda: Oriental Institute, 1938, no. 79).
5. Edward Sell, *Studies*, p. 226.
6. Arthur Jeffery, *Materials for the History of the Text of the Quran* (New York: Russell F. Moore, 1952).
7. Dashti, *23 Years*, p. 28; Mandudi, *Meaning of the Quran*, pp. 17-18; McClintock and Strong, *Cyclopedia*, V:152.
8. Guillaume, *Islam*, p. 189.
9. One example would be Saleh al-Wahaihu, "A Study of Seven Quranic Variants," *International Journal of Islamic and Arabic Studies*, vol. V (1989), no. 2, pp. 1-57.
10. Jeffery, *Materials*, p. 10, no. 2.
11. Ibid., p. 9.
12. McClintock and Strong, *Cyclopedia*, V:152.
13. *Shorter Encyclopedia of Islam*, pp. 278-282; Guillaume, *Islam*, p. 191; Wherry, *A Comprehensive Commentary on the Quran*, pp. 110-111.
14. John Burton, *The Collection of the Quran* (London: Cambridge University Press, 1977), pp. 117ff. See also Arthur Jeffery, *Islam: Muhammad and His Religion* (New York: Liberal Arts Press, 1958), pp. 66-68.
15. Burton, *Collection*, p. 231.
16. Dashti, *23 Years*, p. 98.
17. E.M. Wherry, *A Comprehensive Commentary on the Quran*, p. 110.
18. Canon Sell, *Historical Development of the Quran* (Madras: Diocesan Press, 1923), pp. 36-37.
19. Jeffery, *Materials*, pp. 5-6. See also Caesar Farah, *Islam: Beliefs and Observations* (New York, Barrons, 1987), 28.
20. Ibid.
21. Caesar Farah, *Islam: Beliefs and Observations* (New York: Barrons, 1987), p. 28.
22. *Shorter Encyclopedia of Islam*, p. 271.
23. Sell, *Studies*, p. 208.
24. McClintock and Strong, *Cyclopedia*, V:152.
25. *Concise Encyclopedia of Islam*, p. 228.

Chapter 10—A Scientific Examination of the Quran

1. Maurice Bucaille, *The Bible, the Quran and Science* (Indianapolis: American Trust

Pub., 1979), p. 126. He has been answered in a definitive way by Dr. William Campbell in a book soon to be published by Arab World Ministries in Upper Darby, Pennsylvania. He was kind enough to allow us to read his unpublished manuscript.

2. For a short discussion of this point, see Adelphi Ghiyathuddin and Ernest Hahn, *The Integrity of the Bible According to the Quran and the Hadith* (Hyderabad, India: Henry Martyn Institute of Islamic Studies, 1977). John Gilchrist, *The Textual History of the Quran and the Bible* (Benoni, South Africa: Jesus to the Muslims, 1987). For a lengthy discussion see: C.G. Pfander, *The Balance of Truth* (London: Religious Tract Society, 1910).

3. Selim Abdul-Ahad and Ernest Hahn, *The Gospel of Barnabas* (Hyderabad, India: Henry Martyn Institute of Islamic Studies, 1985).

    William Campbell, *The Gospel of Barnabas: Its True Value* (Rawalpinidi, Pakistan: Christian Study Center, 1989). John Gilchrist, *Origins and Sources of the Gospel of Barnabas* (Benoni, South Africa: Jesus to the Muslims, 1987).

4. For a complete list of contradictions between the Quran and the Gospel of Barnabas, see Campbell, Abdul-Ahad, and Hahn listed above.

5. For a short treatment on the subject see John Gilchrist, *The Crucifixion: A Fact, Not a Fiction* (Benoni, South Africa: Jesus to the Muslims, 1987). For a lengthy treatment, see Josh McDowell and John Gilchrist, *The Islam Debate* (San Bernardino, CA: Here's Life Pub., 1983) and Anis Shorrosh, *Islam Revealed* (Nashville: Thomas Nelson, 1988).

6. *Encyclopedia Britannica*, 13:479.

7. Sell, *Studies*, p. 225.

8. C.G. Pfander, *Balance of Truth*, pp. 283ff.

9. Caesar Farah, *Islam: Beliefs and Observations* (New York: Barrons, 1987), pp. 86ff.

10. Guillaume, *Islam*, pp. 21ff.

11. *Encyclopedia Britannica*, 15:479.

12. Ibid., p.763.

13. *Concise Dictionary of Islam*, p. 229.

14. McClintock and Strong, *Cyclopedia*, VI:407. See also Dashti, *23 Years*, p. 92.

15. Dashti, *23 Years*, pp. 82ff.

16. For the documentation on the sources of the Quran, see the books listed in the bibliography under such names as Jeffery, Katsh, Tisdall, Gibb, Bell, Sell, Muir, Guillaume, Preserved Smith, Pfander, Shorrosh, Sweetman, Seale, Zwemer, as well as the standard reference works such as encyclopedias and dictionaries on Islam.

17. Ibid., p. 51.

18. Dashti has an interesting discussion of the jinn on pp. 158ff. See also Rudolph Frieling, *Christianity and Islam: A Battle for the True Image of Man* (Edinburgh: Flores Books, 1980), p. 40ff.

19. *The Concise Dictionary of Islam*, p. 229; Jomier, *The Bible and the Quran* (Henry Regency Co., Chacago, 1959), 59ff.; Sell, *Studies*, pp. 210ff.; Guillaume, *Islam*, p. 13.

20. *Encyclopedia Britannica*, 15:648.

21. Richard Bell, *Introduction to the Quran*, pp. 163ff. See also: Bell, *The Origin of Islam in Its Christian Environment*, pp. 110ff., 139ff.; Sell, *Studies*, pp. 216ff. See also Tisdall and Pfander.

22. *Encyclopedia of Islam* (ed. Eliade), pp. 303ff.; *International Standard Bible Encyclopedia*, pp. 1:219ff.

23. See Sell, *Studies*, pp. 219ff. for details.

24. Guillaume, *Islam*, pp. 38ff.; Jeffery, A., "Anti-Christian Literature," *Muslim World*, vol. 17 (1927) pp. 216-219. Kenneth Cragg, *The Call of the Minaret*, pp. 254-264, 286-291. See also Cragg's work, *The House of Islam*.

25. *Concise Dictionary of Islam*, pp. 229ff.; H Becker, *Christianity and Islam*, pp. 21ff.

26. Richard Bell, *Introduction to the Quran*, p. 141.

            ,opedia Britannica, 12:708.

            ,ncise Dictionary of Islam, pp. 229-230.

     . Ibid., p. 2.

30. Victor Khalil and Deborah Khalil, "When Christians Meet Muslims," *Christian Herald*, July/August 1988, p. 44.

Appendix C—The Moon God and Archeology

1. Ahmed Deedat, *What Is His Name?* (Durban, S.A.: IPCI, 1990). Deedat argues that "Allah" is a biblical name for God on the basis of "Allelujah" which he convolutes into "Allah-lujah" (p. 37). This only reveals that he does not understand Hebrew. The divine name is the "jah" preceded by the verb "to praise." His other "biblical" arguments are equally absurd. He also claims that the word "Allah" was never corrupted by paganism. "Allah is a unique word for the only God . . . you cannot make a feminine of Allah" (p. 32). He does not tell his readers that one of Allah's daughters was named "Al-Lat," which is the feminine form of "Allah."

2. Mark Hall, *A Study of the Sumerian Moon-god, Nanna / Suen*, Ph.D., 1985, University of PA.

3. Austin Potts, *The Hymns and Prayers to the Moon-god, Sin*, Ph.D., 1971, Dropsie College, p. 2.

4. Ibid., p. 4.

5. Ibid., p. 7.

6. Ibid., pp. 14-21.

7. Yigal, Yadin, *Hazor* (New York: Random House, 1975; London: Oxford, 1972; Jerusalem: Magnes, 1958).

8. Carleton S. Coon, *Southern Arabia* (Washington, D.C.: Smithsonian, 1944), p. 398.

9. North Arabian archeological finds concerning Al-Lat are discussed in: Isaac Rabinowitz, "Aramaic Inscriptions of the Fifth Century" (JNES, XV [1956], 1-9); "Another Aramaic Record of the North Arabian goddess Han'Llat" (JNES, XVIII [1959], 154-55).

    Edward Linski, "The goddess Atirat in Ancient Arabia, in Babylon and in Ugarit: Her Relation to the Moon-god and the Sungoddess" (Orientalia Lovaniensia Periodica, 3; 101-09).

    H.J. Drijvers, "Iconography and Character of the Arab goddess Allat," found in *Etudes Preliminaries Aux Religions Orientales Dans L'Empire Roman* (ed. by Maarten J. Verseren [Leiden: Brill, 1978], pp. 331-51).

10. Berta Segall, "The Iconography of Cosmic Kingship" (*The Art Bulletin*, vol. xxxviii, 1956), p. 77.

11. G. Caton Thompson, *The Tombs and Moon Temple of Hureidha* (Oxford: Oxford University Press, 1944).

12. See Richard Le Baron Bower, Jr., and Frank P. Albright, *Archeological Discoveries in South Arabia* (Baltimore: Johns Hopkins University Press, 1958), p. 78ff.; Ray Cleveland, *An Ancient Southern Arabian Necropolis* (Baltimore: John Hopkins University Press, 1965); Nelson Gleuck, *Deities and Dolphins* (New York: Farrar, Strauss and Giroux, 1965).

13. Coon, *Southern Arabia*, p. 399.

14. Ibid.

15. *Three Early Christian-Muslim Debates* (ed. by N.A. Newman [Hatfield, PA: I.B.R.I., 1994], pp. 357, 413, 426).

16. Ibid., p. 719.

17. Caesar Farah, *Islam: Beliefs and Observations* (New York: Barrons, 1987), p. 28.

General Bibliography

Selim Abdul-Ahad and W. Gairdner, *The Gospel of Barnabas: An Inquiry* (Henry Martyn Institute Of Islamic Studies, Hyderabad, India, 1985).

Ghiyathuddin Adelphi and Ernest Hahn, *The Integrity of the Bible According to the Quran and the Hadith* (Henry Martyn Institute Of Islamic Studies, Hyderabad, India, 1977).

Frank Albright and Richard Bowen, *Archeological Discoveries in South Arabia* (Baltimore, 1958).

Michael Nazir-Ali, *Islam: A Christian Perspective* (The Westminster Press, Philadelphia, 1983).

Maulna Muhammad, *Ali, A Manual of Hadith* (The Ahmadyya Anjuman Ishaat Islam, Lahore, n.d.).

Yusuf Ali, *The Holy Quran* (Amana Corp., Brentwood, Maryland, 1983).

Approaches to Islam in Religious Studies, ed. Richard Martin (University of Arizona Press, Tucson, 1985).

Arthur J. Arberry, *The Koran* (Oxford University Press, Oxford, 1989).

Ulfat Aziz-us-samad, *Islam and Christianity* (Begum Aisha Bawany Waqf, Karachi, 1970).

Giullo Basetti-Sani, *The Koran in the Light of Christ* (Fransiscan Herald Press, Chicago, 1977).

N.J. Dawood, *The Koran: Translated with Notes* (Penguin Books, Baltimore, 1974).

J.H. Bavinck, *The Church Between the Temple and the Mosque* (Wm. B. Eerdmans Pub. Co., Grand Rapids, n.d.).

Carl Becker, *Christianity and Islam* (Harper & Row, New York, 1909).

Richard Bell, *Bell's Introduction to the Quran* (Edinburgh University Press, Edinburgh, 1953).

_____ , *The Origin of Islam in its Christian Environment* (MacMillan, London, 1926).

M. Bravmann, *The Spiritual Background of Early Islam* (E.J. Brill, Leiden, 1972).

Essad Bey, *Mohammed* (Longman, Green & Co., New York, 1936).

David Brown, *The Cross of the Messiah* (Sheldon Press, London, 1969).

John Burton, *The Collection of the Quran* (Cambridge University Press, London, 1977).

William Campbell, *The Gospel of Barnabas: Its True Value* (Christian Study Center, Rawalpinidi, Pakistan, 1989).

Christian Witness Among Muslims (Henry Martyn Institute of Islamic Studies, Hyderabad, India, 1987).

The Concise Encyclopedia of Islam, ed. Cyril Classe (Stacey Inter., London, 1989).

Controversial Tracts on Christianity and Mahometanism by Henry Martyn, eds. Samuel and Lee (J. Smith, Cambridge, 1824).

ɾagg, *The Call of the Minaret* (Oxford University Press, New York, 1956).

_____ , *The Event of the Quran* (Allen and Unwin, London, 1971).

_____ , *The House of Islam* (Dickenson, Belmont, CA, 1969).

_____ , *The Mind of the Quran* (George Allen and Unwin Ltd., London, 1973).

_____ , *Sandals at the Mosque: Christian Presence Amid Islam* (Oxford University Press, New York, 1959).

Norman Daniel, *Islam and the West* (Edinburgh University Press, Edinburgh, 1966).

Ali Dashti, *23 Years: A Study of the Prophetic Career of Mohammed* (George Allen & Unwin, London, 1985).

El Dessuky, *A Short History of the Life of the Prophet Muhammad* (Uganda Pub. House, Kampala, 1971).

R.F. Dibble, *Mohammed* (The Viking Press, New York, 1926).

James Dretke, *A Christian Approach to Muslims* (William Carey Library, London, 1979).

Early Islam, ed. Desmond Stewart (Time, Inc., New York, 1967).

Encyclopedia Britannica (Encyclopedia Britannica, Inc., London, 1957).

Encyclopedia of Islam, eds. Gibb, Levi-Provencal, Schacht (E.J. Brill, Leiden, 1960).

Encyclopedia of Islam, eds. Houtsma, Arnold, Basset, Hartman (E.J. Brill, Leiden, 1913.)

Encyclopedia of Religion, ed. Mercea Eliade (MacMillan Pub. Co., New York, 1987).

Encyclopedia of Religion, eds. Paul Meagher, Thomas O'Brian, Consuela Aherne (Corpus Pub., Washington D.C., 1979).

Encyclopedia of Religion and Ethics, ed. James Hastings (T. & T. Clark, Edinburgh, 1908).

The Facts on File: Encyclopedia of World Mythology and Legend, ed. Anthony Mercatane (Facts on File, New York, 1983).

Caesar Farah, *Islam: Beliefs and Observations* (Barrons, New York, 1987).

Sydney Fisher, *The Middle East: A History* (Alfred Knopf, New York, 1969).

Rudolph Frieling, *Christianity and Islam: A Battle for the True Image of Man* (Floris Books, Edinburgh, 1978).

C. George Fry and James King, *Islam: A Survey of the Muslim Faith* (Baker, Grand Rapids, 1980).

Helmut Gatje, *The Quran and Its Exegesis* (University of California Press, Los Angeles, 1976).

John Gilchrist, *Christ in Islam and Christianity* (Jesus to the Muslims, Benoni, South Africa, 1987).

_____ , *The Crucifixion of Christ: A Fact, Not Fiction* (Jesus to the Muslims, Benoni, South Africa, 1987).

_____ , *Is Muhammad Foretold in the Bible?* (Jesus to the Muslims, Benoni, South Africa, 1987).

_____ , *Jam' Al-Qur'an: The Codification of the Quran Text* (Jesus to the Muslims, Benoni, South Africa, 1989).

_____, *Origins and Sources of the Gospel of Barnabas* (Jesus to the Muslims, Benoni, South Africa, 1987).

_____, *The Textual History of the Quran and the Bible* (Jesus to the Muslims, Benoni, South Africa, 1987).

_____, *What Indeed Was the Sign of Jonah?* (Jesus to the Muslims, Benoni, South Africa, 1987).

H.A.R. Gibb, *Mohammedanism: An Historical Survey* (Mentor Books, New York, 1955).

_____, "Pre-Islamic Monotheism in Arabia," in *Harvard Theological Review*, vol. 55, 1962.

John Glubb, *The Life and Times of Muhammad* (Stein and Day, New York, 1970).

Martin Goldsmith, *Islam and Christian Witness* (InterVarsity Press, Downers Grove, IL, 1982).

Alfred Guillaume, *Islam* (Penguin Books, London, 1954).

_____, *New Light on the Life of Muhammad* (Manchester University Press, Manchester, n.d.).

_____, *The Traditions of Islam* (Clarendon Press, London, 1924).

Ernest Hahn, *Jesus in Islam* (Henry Martyn Institute Of Islamic Studies, Hyderabad, India, 1987).

_____, *Understanding Some Muslim Misunderstandings* (Fellowship of Faith, Toronto, 1983).

Abdul Hamed, *Islam and Christianity* (Carlton Press, New York, 1967).

Mahmoud Hoballah, *Muhammad the Prophet* (The Islamic Center, Washington D.C., n.d.).

Muhammad Husayn Haykal, *The Life of Muhammad* (Crescent Pub. Co., Delhi, 1976).

Thomas Hughes, *A Dictionary of Islam* (Allen & Co., London, 1885).

Muhammed Hamidullah, *Introduction to Islam* (Centre Culturel Islamique, Paris, 1957).

C. Hurgronji, *Mohammedanism* (Hyperion Press, Westport, CT, 1981).

International Journal of Middle East Studies.

International Journal of Islamic and Arabic Studies.

Ibraham Ishak, *Black Gold and Holy War* (Thomas Nelson, Nashville, 1983).

Islam and Christianity; Or, The Quran and the Bible; A Letter to a Muslim Friend, By a Missionary (American Tract Society, New York, 1901).

Islam: The First & Final Religion (Begum Aisha Bawany Waqf, Karachi, 1978).

Toshihikio Izutsu, *Ethico-Religious Concepts on the Quran* (McGill University Press, Montreal, 1966).

Arthur Jeffery, "Anti-Christian Literature," in *Muslim World*, vol. 17, 1927.

_____, *The Foreign Vocabulary of the Quran* (Baroda: Oriental Institute, 1938).

_____*Islam: Muhammad and His Religion* (The Liberal Arts Press, New York, 1958).

_____, *Materials for the History of the Text of the Quran* (E.J. Brill, Leiden, 1937).

666

_____ , *The Quran as Scripture* (Russell F. Moore, New York, 1952).

_s Jomier, *The Bible and the Quran* (Henry Regency Co., Chicago, 1959).

_urnal of Semitic Studies.

Abraham Katsh, *Judaism in Islam: Biblical and Talmudic Backgrounds of the Koran and Its Commentaries* (New York University Press, New York, 1954).

Badru Kateregga and David Shenk, *Islam and Christianity* (Wm. B., Eerdmans Pub. Co., Grand Rapids, 1980).

Muhammad Kutub, *Islam: The Misunderstood Religion* (International Islamic Federation of Student Organizations, Kuwait, 1982).

Abdullah Mandudi, *The Meaning of the Quran* (Islamic Pub. Ltd., Lahore, 1967).

C.R. Marsh, *Share Your Faith with a Muslim* (Moody Press, Chicago, 1975).

John McClintock and James Strong, *Cyclopedia of Biblical, Theological, and Ecclesiastical Literature* (Baker, Grand Rapids, 1981).

Josh McDowell and John Gilchrist, *The Islam Debate* (Here's Life Pub., San Bernardino, CA, 1983).

Henry Mercier, *The Koran* (Luzac & Co., London, 1956).

William Miller, *A Christian's Response to Islam* (Presbyterian & Reformed, Phillipsburg, NJ, 1976).

G.E. Morrison, *The Christian Approach to the Muslim* (Edinburgh House Press, London, 1959).

William Muir, *The Life of Mohammed from Original Sources* (John Grant, London, 1923).

_____ , *Some of the Sources of the Coran (n.p., London, 1901).*

Muslim-Christian Conflicts, eds. Joseph Saud and Barbara Pillsbury (Western Press, Boulder, CO, 1978).

Kausar, Nazir, *Islam & the West* (Muhammad Ashraf, Karachi, 1976).

Phil Parshall, *Bridges to Islam* (Baker, Grand Rapids, 1985).

John Penrice, *A Dictionary and Glossary of the Koran* (Biblo and Tanner, New York, 1969).

C.G. Pfander, *Balance of Truth* (The Religious Tract Society, London, 1910).

Marmaduke Pickthall, *The Meaning of the Glorious Koran* (New American Library, New York, n.d.).

Sayyid Qutb, *Islam: The Religion of the Future* (International Islamic Federation of Student Organizations, Kuwait, n.d.).

_____ , *This Religion of Islam* (International Islamic Federation of Student Organizations, Kuwait, 1982).

Canon Sell and David Maroliouth, "Christ in Mohammedan Literature," in James Hastings, ed., *Dictionary of Christ and the Gospels* (Charles Scribners' Sons, New York, 1917).

Canon Sell, *Historical Development of the Quran* (Diocesan Press, Madras, 1923).

_____ , *The Life of Muhammad* (Christian Literature Society of India, Lahore, 1913).

_____, *Studies in Islam* (Diocesan Press, London, 1928).

M.S. Seale, *Quran and Bible* (Croom Helm, London, 1978).

Shorter Encyclopedia of Islam, eds. H. Gibb and J. Kramers (Cornell University Press, Ithaca, NY, 1953).

Anis Shorrosh, *Islam Revealed* (Thomas Nelson Pub., Nashville, 1988).

Henry Preserved Smith, *The Bible and Islam; or, The Influence of the Old and New Testaments on the Religion of Mohammed* (Charles Scribners' Sons, New York, 1897).

Salomon Reinach, *Orpheus: A History of Religion* (Liveright, Inc., New York, 1932).

Jane Smith, *An Historical and Semitic Study of the Term Islam As Seen in a Sequence of Quran Commentaries* (University of Montana for Harvard University dissertations, 1970).

Percy Smith, "Did Jesus Foretell Amed?" in *Muslim World*, vol. 12, 1922.

H. Spencer, *Islam and the Gospel of God* (S.P.C.K., Madras, 1956).

Henry Stanton, *The Teaching of the Quran* (Biblo and Tanner, New York, 1969).

James Sweetman, *The Bible in Islam* (British & Foreign Society, London, 1953).

William Tisdall, *A Manual of the Leading Muhammadan Objections to Christianity* (S.P.C.K., London, 1911).

_____, *Original Sources of Islam* (T. & T. Clark, Edinburgh, 1901).

_____, *The Religion of the Crescent; Being the James Long Lectures on Muhammadanism* (S.P.C.K., London, 1910).

W. Montgomery Watt, *Companion to the Quran* (George Allen & Unwin Ltd., London, 1967).

_____, "Belief in a 'High God' in Pre-Islamic Mecca," in *Journal of Semitic Studies*, vol. 16, 1971.

_____, *Muhammad at Mecca* (Clarendon Press, Oxford, 1953).

_____, *Muhammad at Medina* (Clarendon Press, Oxford, 1956).

E.M. Wherry, *A Comprehensive Commentary on the Quran* (Otto Zeller Verlag, Osnabruck, 1973).

Edward Westermarck, *Pagan Survivals in Mohammedan Civilization* (Philo Press, Amsterdam, 1933).

Don Wismer, *The Islamic Jesus* (Garland Pub., New York, 1977).

Bat Ye'or, *The Dhimmi: Jews and Christians Under Islam* (Fairleigh Dickinson University Press, Rutherford, NJ, 1985).

Samuel Zwemer, *Across the World of Islam: Studies in Aspects of the Mohammedan Faith and in the Present Awaking of the Moslem Multitudes* (Fleming Revell, New York, 1929).

_____, *The Cross Above the Crescent* (Zondervan Pub. Co., Grand Rapids, 1941).

_____, *Islam: A Challenge to Faith* (Student Volunteer Movement for Foreign Missions, New York, 1908).

_____, *The Moslem Doctrines of God; An Essay on the Character and Attributes of Allah According to the Koran* (American Tract Society, New York, 1905).